M000250127

Patricia Cranton

1949–2016

Patricia Cranton earned one of the highest civilian honors her country has to bestow, the Order of Canada, in 2016, and was inducted into the International Adult Continuing Education Hall of Fame in 2014. But she was so much more than awards and honors can convey, as all who knew her can attest. It was a pleasure and a privilege to work with her over the years, and I know that people all over the world will mourn her loss, as I do. We are fortunate that her work, like her memory, lives on. I am especially grateful that we have this new edition of her classic book, *Understanding and Promoting Transformative Learning*, to remind us of her unique voice and ever-evolving thought.

David Brightman
Senior Editor, Higher Education
Stylus Publishing, LLC.

UNDERSTANDING AND PROMOTING TRANSFORMATIVE LEARNING

UNDERSTANDING AND PROMOTING TRANSFORMATIVE LEARNING

A Guide to Theory and Practice

Patricia Cranton

Third Edition

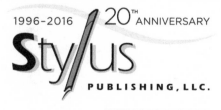

1996–2016 20TH ANNIVERSARY

Stylus
PUBLISHING, LLC.

STERLING, VIRGINIA

Published by Stylus Publishing, LLC.
22883 Quicksilver Drive
Sterling, Virginia 20166-2102

Library of Congress Cataloging-in-Publication Data
Names: Cranton, Patricia.
Title: Understanding and promoting transformative learning: a
guide to theory and practice / Patricia Cranton.
Description: Third edition. | Sterling, Virginia: Stylus Publishing,
[2016] |
Includes bibliographical references and index.
Identifiers: LCCN 2015051160 (print) |
LCCN 2016000287 (ebook) |
  ISBN 9781620364116 (cloth : alk. paper) |
  ISBN 9781620364123 (pbk. : alk. paper) |
  ISBN 9781620364130 (library networkable e-edition) |
  ISBN 9781620364147 (consumer e-edition)
Subjects: LCSH: Adult learning. | Transformative learning. |
Transfer of training. | Adult education.
Classification: LCC LC5225.L42 C72 2016 (print) |
LCC LC5225.L42 (ebook) | DDC 374--dc23
LC record available at http://lccn.loc.gov/2015051160

13-digit ISBN: 978-1-62036-411-6 (cloth)
13-digit ISBN: 978-1-62036-412-3 (paperback)
13-digit ISBN: 978-1-62036-413-0 (library networkable e-edition)
13-digit ISBN: 978-1-62036-414-7 (consumer e-edition)

Printed in the United States of America

All first editions printed on acid-free paper
that meets the American National Standards Institute
Z39-48 Standard.

Bulk Purchases

Quantity discounts are available for use in workshops and for
staff development.
Call 1-800-232-0223

First Edition, 2016

Dedicated to the memory of Jack and Edee Mezirow

CONTENTS

PREFACE TO THE THIRD EDITION

Interest in transformative learning has spiraled since Jack Mezirow's (1978, 1981) early works on perspective transformation, and interest continues to grow as the theory itself is changing, developing, and incorporating a variety of perspectives. The 2014 XI International Transformative Learning Conference was held at Teachers College, Columbia University. Representing 18 countries, 294 participants from a variety of disciplines (e.g., higher education, social justice, adult education, workplace education, and the arts) attended the conference. The conference paid tribute to the passing of Jack and Edee Mezirow and celebrated Jack's contributions by creating and presenting the Jack Mezirow Living Theory Award.

The *Journal of Transformative Education,* established in 2003, continues to thrive and expand its offerings in response to theoretical developments. In addition, articles on transformative learning regularly appear in journals such as *Adult Education Quarterly* and the *New Directions for Continuing and Adult Education* series. Most texts devoted to providing an overview of the adult education field contain a section on transformative learning.

Background

Historically, adult education has been seen as a political movement—a movement toward freedom and liberation that is both personal and social. During the 1970s and 1980s, theorists, writers, and practitioners tended to focus on a humanistic approach to adult education, guided in large part by the influential writings of Malcolm Knowles. This began to change in the 1990s as the attention of scholars in higher and adult education started to shift back to ideology critique and social change. Well into the 2000s, we have seen ideology critique taking its place in research, theory, and practice without displacing the more humanistic approaches; this trend toward an integrated unified theory of transformative learning is growing (Cranton & Taylor, 2012). Brookfield's writings (2005, 2012) have been influential in the United States, and the work of Nesbit, Brigham, Taber, and Gibb (2013) leads the way in Canada.

The traditional definition of *transformative learning* is a process that leads to a deep shift in perspective during which habits of mind become more open, more permeable, more discriminating, and better justified (Cranton, 2006; Mezirow, 2000). To move toward a more integrated definition, the process can be rational (cognitive), extrarational (e.g., intuitive, spiritual, relational, and emotional), and/or focused on social change and social justice. Different individuals may engage in transformative learning in different ways; the same individual may engage in transformative learning in different ways in different contexts.

Need

Resources and advice for practitioners continue to be somewhat limited. E. W. Taylor and Snyder (2012) have pointed out that the research that frames pedagogy is growing and that there is an increased interest from educators in disciplines outside of education who are looking for a guide to practice. How can transformative learning be encouraged in classrooms? In the workplace? In informal self-help groups? In community development initiatives? We need to pay attention to how to support and create the environment that might foster transformative learning in our practice. Clearly, transformative learning is of increasing importance in the field, but we have fallen behind in helping practitioners see how the theory can be relevant in their work.

Purpose and Audience

The first and second editions of *Understanding and Promoting Transformative Learning* were intended to explain transformative learning theory and describe the process from the learner's perspective, exploring individual differences in transformative learning and presenting practical strategies for fostering transformative learning, while emphasizing that adult educators themselves are transformative learners.

The primary purpose of the third edition remains essentially the same as that of previous editions. I incorporate recent theoretical developments such as John Dirkx's (2012) Jungian approach to transformative learning and nurturing soul, N. K. Charaniya's (2012) ideas about the role of imagination and spirituality in transformation, Mary Belenky and Ann Stanton's (Belenky & Stanton, 2000) idea of connected knowing, and Stephen Brookfield's (2012) thoughts on ideology critique.

Throughout the book, I focus on providing a practical and accessible approach. I have taught courses on transformative learning at the bachelor's, master's, and doctoral levels for more than 20 years. These experiences have given me a good sense of how to communicate with potential readers.

The intended audiences of the third edition of *Understanding and Promoting Transformative Learning* remain the same as for the first and second editions: faculty members and graduate students in adult and higher education, professional developers in higher education and other settings, and adult education practitioners working in a variety of contexts. The third edition will help educators understand what transformative learning is, distinguish it from other forms of learning, and foster it in their practice. The first half of the book is dedicated to clarifying transformative learning theory and relating it to other theoretical frameworks. I examine transformative learning from the learner's perspective, and I discuss individual differences in how learners go through the process. In the second half of the book, the focus is squarely on strategies for promoting transformative learning in a variety of contexts. Practitioners will be able to take ideas from the text and apply them directly in their teaching.

Overview of the Contents

The general organization of the third edition of *Understanding and Promoting Transformative Learning* remains the same as that of the second edition. Chapter 1, "The Context of Transformative Learning," provides an overview of perspectives on learning in higher and adult education and places transformative learning within that context. I follow both Jürgen Habermas's and Jack Mezirow's categorizations of instrumental, communicative, and emancipatory learning to do this.

Chapter 2, "The Origins of Transformative Learning Theory," describes the original theory as developed by Mezirow, including the updates that have occurred over the last 20 years. In order to do this, I draw on Lisa Baumgartner's (2012) "Mezirow's Theory of Transformative Learning from 1975 to Present," which was published in *The Handbook of Transformative Learning*. I describe content, process, and premise reflection in this chapter.

In Chapter 3, "Transformative Learning Theory as an Integrated Perspective," I elaborate on Mezirow's traditional theory by reviewing the extrarational approach to understanding transformative learning, describing connected and relational learning, examining social change as a goal of transformative learning, considering transformative learning in the context of groups and organizations, and outlining the ecological view of the theory.

In Chapter 4, "Transformation: The Learner's Story," I describe the process undergone by learners as they are engaged in transformation. In Chapter 5, "Individual Differences," I suggest that individuals experience transformative learning in different ways based on my understanding of Jung's psychological type theory.

Next, I turn to practical strategies for adult educators who hope to foster transformative learning. In Chapter 6, "Educator Roles," I present educator roles within the framework of instrumental, communicative, and emancipatory learning. In a discussion of power, I include Foucault's conceptualization of power—an understanding of power that Brookfield has made accessible to educators. I also incorporate some thoughts on educator authenticity. I refer readers to Dan Pratt and John Collins's (2014) Teaching Perspectives Inventory to help practitioners understand their preferences for a variety of educator roles in higher and adult education.

Chapter 7, "The Importance of Power," expands on the notion of empowerment; I incorporate the newer thinking about how educators and learners exercise power. The chapter provides practical strategies for empowering learners.

In Chapter 8, "Fostering Critical Self-Reflection and Self-Awareness," I include ideas for stimulating critical reflection and critical self-reflection, and I also pay attention to the intuitive and affective aspects of how we question our assumptions, beliefs, and perspectives. I discuss the way the strategies address the variety of threads inherent in an integrative perspective on transformative learning (e.g., arts-based strategies, intuitive strategies, relational learning, and narrative learning).

In Chapter 9, "Supporting Transformative Learning," I suggest that the educator who fosters transformative learning has a moral responsibility to provide and arrange for support for his or her students. I suggest a number of ways in which support can be given, both within and outside of the learner group.

Finally, in Chapter 10, "The Educator's Transformative Process," I discuss the process educators may go through as they experience transformative learning in relation to their practice. Included is a description, based on my research, of how educator authenticity develops with experience and how becoming more authentic is a transformative process.

ACKNOWLEDGMENTS

I am indebted to David Brightman (senior editor, higher education) for his many years of ongoing support and encouragement.

I especially want to thank McKenzie Baker who gently guided me through proofreading and copyediting with great skill.

It is with deep gratitude that I acknowledge the insights of Laurence Robert Cohen through both our conversations and his wide-ranging comments on the manuscript.

I also appreciate my furry family, who once again patiently put up with delayed snacks and walks while I stared at the computer screen.

I

THE CONTEXT OF
TRANSFORMATIVE
LEARNING

Educators, especially those interested in transformative learning, struggle to define the boundaries and the scope of their discipline. Transformative learning is a relatively new field, though I wonder how long we can continue to say that. Still, if we think about the existence of graduate programs in a field, adult education in general is a recent discipline, and transformative learning is even more recent. We are still struggling with who we are, but in the last 20 years, research has proliferated, and theory development has reached a new maturity.

It is my purpose in this chapter not so much to review the different ways in which adult learning is described, but rather to create the boundaries around transformative learning theory and to situate transformative learning theory within the more general literature on learning in adult education, higher education, and professional education. When I teach courses and facilitate workshops on transformative learning, we inevitably come to a point in our discussions where everything seems transformative. Someone will say, "But if I learn a new computer skill, that frees me to do things in a new way and I feel transformed," or another person will say, "Learning to read is a skill, but it opens up the world," and almost always, people will begin to argue that children can engage in transformative learning. When a young person rebels against parental rules, is that not critical reflection? It takes us some time to work our way out of these dilemmas in our conversation. We deconstruct and then reconstruct the meaning of the theory. Perhaps what I can do in this chapter is to work through some of that process and at least clarify the perspective on transformative learning on which this book is based.

1

Essentially, I follow Mezirow's (2012) definition of *transformative learning* as a process by which previously uncritically assimilated assumptions, beliefs, values, and perspectives are questioned and thereby become more open, permeable, and better validated. However, I have been strongly influenced by the work of my colleagues who incorporate imagination, intuition, soul, and affect into their understanding of the process (Dirkx, 2012). I have become interested in exploring a more integrated or unified theory of transformative learning (Cranton & Taylor, 2012), one in which the alternative perspectives in the literature can be brought together to form a more comprehensive understanding of transformative learning theory. But first, I focus on situating transformative learning in the broader context of adult learning.

Adult Learning as a Distinctive Process

Regardless of the context, adult learners are mature, socially responsible individuals who participate in sustained informal or formal activities that lead them to acquire new knowledge, skills, or values; elaborate on existing knowledge, skills, or values; revise their basic beliefs and assumptions; or change the way they see some aspect of themselves or the world around them. A learner might take classes to fulfill requirements in a doctoral program, participate in a training session required by her organization, learn how to ski, or join a bereavement group to understand her reactions to the death of her spouse. Learning in some form is an aspect of virtually every person's life.

Given the complexity of human differences, the diverse contexts within which people live and work, and the many types of things people learn, it seems fruitless to try to delineate general characteristics of adult learning. Yet we seem to want to be able to say that adult learning is different from children's learning, so for decades writers have tried to list those things that make adult learning distinctive. I review some of those characteristics here, though I also question how universal they are.

Adult learning is often considered voluntary. Individuals choose to become involved in either informal or formal learning activities because they want to develop personally or as a response to a professional or practical need. The loss of a job, a change in lifestyle, or a move to a different geographical location may prompt someone to want to learn. When we consider adult learning as voluntary, this leads to the assumption that people are highly motivated and interested in a content that is relevant to their needs, which may or may not be true. Many people feel obligated to attend workplace learning activities, and some may be required to engage in training or retraining. For those who participate in mandated programs, a skilled facilitator or a good course can pique interest, and even when people do choose to become involved in learning, their interest may flag for a variety of reasons.

Adult learning is also often described as self-directed. The concept of self-directed learning has permeated adult education theory and practice to such an extent that it is almost equated with adult education. Unfortunately, the definitions of *self-directed learning* are varied and confusing. It was Knowles (1975, 1980) who started this when he suggested that all adults have a preference for being self-directed. The term *preference* was overlooked, and educators assumed learners were self-directed. Knowles saw self-directed learning as a process by which people made the instructional design decisions—identifying their needs, setting their own goals, choosing how to learn, gathering materials, finding resources, and judging their progress. Knowles felt that this was a distinguishing characteristic of adult learning. It was by no means intended to be an independent or isolating way of learning; however, in some of its applications it became so. Over the years, self-direction came to mean a characteristic of a person (similar to autonomy), a method of teaching, a developmental goal, and several other variations on these themes. In 1991, Candy sorted out the literature up to that point and developed a helpful framework. He described the following facets of self-direction: (a) learner control (people making decisions about their learning within a formal context), (b) autonomy (a personal characteristic), (c) self-management (planning one's educational experiences), and (d) autodidaxy (engaging in informal, independent learning projects). In recent years, there have been few developments in our understanding of self-directed learning. Knowles's original conceptualization has remained the standard by which we describe the characteristics of self-directed learners and the processes of engaging in self-directed learning. It is important to note, however, that we cannot assume that adults are automatically self-directed.

Many writers have proposed that adult learning should be practical or experiential in nature, an idea that began with Dewey (1938) and has stayed with us over the decades. This conceptualization is based on the assumption that adults have immediate problems to solve and that they wish to apply their learning directly to their workplaces or to their personal lives. Kolb (1984, 2015) has elaborated on and contributed to the role of experiential learning in adult education. It is now standard practice that educators make every effort to include real-life applications in their programs. Acting on learning (or sometimes *transfer of learning*, defined as application in the world outside of the classroom) is often described as the goal of education. Mezirow (2003a) suggested that transformation has not taken place until an individual has acted on the learning. MacKeracher (2012) explicitly discussed the role of experience in transformative learning and illustrated this process through a case study of her own experiences, including learning to be a teacher, learning to be self-directed, learning to be a professor, and learning to be retired. However, as I propose in Chapter 5, people may vary on the extent to which they value practical learning and experiential activities.

Humanism has strongly influenced adult education; Knowles, who defined *adult education* in the 1970s and the early 1980s, was a student of Carl Rogers, a scholar well known for client-centered therapy. Later, Knowles was criticized for his humanistic approach (Brookfield, 1986), but Knowles's legacy continues to inform the field. As a result of the influence of humanism, we tend to see adult education as particularly collaborative and participatory. Sitting in a circle, working in groups, and interacting with others are hallmarks of adult education practice. Educators describe themselves as facilitators rather than teachers, and they seek to establish a colearner role with their students. They consider a comfortable and safe atmosphere, both physical and psychological, to be important. As critical theory and postmodernism became integrated into adult and higher education theory, these assumptions were called into question. Early on, Brookfield (2001) used Foucault's understanding of power to point out how many of our traditional collaborative approaches, such as sitting in a circle, lead people to feel vulnerable and exposed, and other techniques, such as keeping a personal journal, actually allow the educator to engage in surveillance or "get into the head" of the participant. Later, he provided a comprehensive discussion of how critical theory informs transformative learning theory (Brookfield, 2012). In this discussion, he emphasized that critical theory focuses "on how adults learn to challenge dominant ideology, uncover power, and contest hegemony" (p. 131). This focus, Brookfield suggested, is crucial for transformative learning to "avoid sliding into an unproblematized focus on the self" (pp. 131–132).

Going back in time again, Knowles (1980), whose work still forms the foundation of much of what we do in adult education today, emphasized the rich *experiences and resources* adults bring to the learning setting. If we disagree with all of the other characteristics that distinguish *andragogy* (defined by Knowles as the art and science of helping adults learn) from pedagogy, we cannot deny that adults have more experience to bring into play than do children. From a constructivist point of view, learners share their experiences and resources with each other to create new knowledge. This tenet fits well with other defining qualities of adult learning—people collaborating voluntarily to construct practical and relevant learning that is, to some extent at least, self-directed. We can question, of course, whether sharing experiences is important to all individuals and whether all types of learning are enhanced by this process.

Self-concept is a term frequently mentioned in relation to adult learning. On one hand, students whose self-understanding is not necessarily positive may find that this inhibits their learning. On the other hand, this can provide a strong motivation for students to grow and learn. The relevance of self-concept is also related to the prevailing notion that the climate of adult classes should be comfortable, safe, and relaxing. Along the same lines, there is the worry that going "back to school," especially engaging in formal educational activities, is *anxiety provoking* for adults. This follows from the assumption that school was a negative experience for many, and a return to this atmosphere brings back the fears of earlier years; however, this is not the case for all students. Another line of reasoning here is that many adults have been away from learning experiences for a number of years and have rusty reading, writing, and time-management skills, which leads them to feel anxious about their ability to succeed. In the last decade or two, as people make more and more shifts in their careers and retraining and professional development become more common, this characteristic may be less defining of *adult learning* than it was in previous times.

Discussions of adult learning almost always include mention of *learning styles*. Those who specialize in higher education and childhood education are also concerned with learning style, so this characteristic is not necessarily specific to one level of education. *Cognitive style* refers to how people acquire, process, store, and use information, and there are a number of different approaches to defining *cognitive style* (Cranton, 2012). *Learning style* consists of a preference for a certain condition or way of learning and is generally considered to be value neutral (MacKeracher, 2004); that is, one style is not better than another. Kolb's (1984, 2015) delineation of *convergers, assimilators, divergers,* and *accommodators* has remained popular over many years. *Convergers*, said Kolb, prefer to arrive quickly at specific, concrete solutions. *Assimilators* like to integrate ideas into models and theories. *Divergers* enjoy generating ideas and working with others. *Accommodators* learn by experience and engage in trial-and-error learning. Any labeling system of this kind has the potential to oversimplify and stereotype, so we need to be careful about how we apply these ideas.

We have been influenced by Gardner's (Gardner, Kornhaber, & Wake, 1996) idea of multiple intelligences (musical, bodily-kinesthetic, logical-mathematical, linguistic, spatial, interpersonal, intrapersonal, and natural), though Gardner has always been clear that he does not view his typology as one of learning styles, rather one of different modalities in which intelligence operates. Similarly, we have Goleman's (1998, 2011) notion of emotional intelligence, which is also seen to be a form of intelligence rather than learning style. Emotional intelligence has to do with a person's ability to manage emotions, recognize emotions in others, and establish good relationships with others.

Some scholars associate learning preferences with gender. For example, MacKeracher (2004), among others, suggested that women prefer relational learning and men autonomous learning. This can also be seen as stereotyping and marginalizing women (English, 2004).

Transformative Learning in Context

How does transformative learning fit within the context of the features of adult learning as they have been presented in the literature over the last two or three decades? I now review the characteristics with an eye specifically turned to transformative learning.

There seems to be no doubt that transformative learning is voluntary. People may not always deliberately set out to critically question their beliefs and values; many times transformative learning is prompted by an outside event, and that event may be unexpected, hurtful, or devastating. Even so, people have the choice of being critically self-reflective or not. In a classroom or other learning environment where the educator has fostering transformative learning as a goal, participants still voluntarily engage in the process. If someone were to mandate transformation or try to force people into the process, I think we would be stepping outside the sphere of transformative learning and into something like brainwashing or indoctrination.

Is transformative learning self-directed? I see the two as interwoven. If we agree that transformative learning is voluntary, as I have just proposed, then a certain amount of self-direction is required for an individual to take the steps of moving into a critical questioning of beliefs, assumptions, and perspectives. People who are completely oppressed may not have the ability to move into this process for all sorts of personal and social reasons. (This is one of the criticisms of Mezirow's work by those who advocate transformative learning as social change.) Mezirow (2000) said that those who are hungry and living in poverty or other extreme social conditions are not likely to participate in transformative learning. Merriam (2004) went so far as to propose that people need a certain level of cognitive development and even a certain level of education. Although these statements are questionable, especially when we are open to processes other than critical self-reflection as central to transformation, it still seems to be the case that transformative learning leads to increased self-direction, so in a way the two go hand in hand. Both are developmental processes.

Being practical or experiential is ostensibly a defining characteristic of adult learning in terms of adults having immediate problems they wish to solve (though I am not sure this is always the case—people come to learning for a variety of reasons); however, transformative learning does not necessarily meet this prerequisite. It is often provoked by an experience, and Kolb (2015) and MacKeracher (2012) saw reflection on experience as a necessary part of learning, but the process itself may be driven by critical *self*-reflection, exploration, and intuition with no further reference to the world outside of the self. This may be especially true for more introverted people (see Chapter 5) and in those times when transformation involves unconscious images and soul work (Dirkx, 2000). Discourse with others may play a vital role, and at times, transformative learning may look like problem solving, but I do not see that it is a practical process. If we follow Mezirow's (2012) thinking, the outcome should be action, but the learning process need not be experiential.

That adult learning in general is seen as participatory and collaborative applies to some extent to transformative learning, depending on how one views the theory. Belenky and Stanton (2000), for example, emphasized conflicts being resolved through dialogue, conversation, storytelling, and perspective sharing. Mezirow (2000, 2012) saw discourse with others as playing an important role in transformative learning. The sharing of experiences and values within a comfortable group atmosphere can obviously act as a stimulant for critical questioning. However, transformation can also occur without collaboration, so I do not think we can describe collaboration as being a defining characteristic of transformative learning.

Transformative learning has to do with making meaning out of experiences and questioning assumptions based on prior experience. Our habitual expectations—what we expect to happen based on what has happened in the past—are the product of experiences, and it is those expectations that are called into question during the transformative learning process. If adult learning is distinguished from childhood learning by the experiences people bring to it, then so can transformative learning be explained as a prerogative of adults. Mezirow (2000, 2012) proposed that it is only in adulthood that people develop the reflective judgment necessary to assess their own reasoning about their habitual expectations.

Self-concept is as relevant to transformative learning as it is to adult learning in general. By definition, *transformative learning* leads to a changed self-perception. When people revise their habits of mind, they are reinterpreting their sense of self in relation to the world. I think of the college trades instructors with whom I work every summer in the Maritimes of Canada. They have returned to school after years and sometimes decades of experience in their trades, and they are in the process of becoming teachers of their trades. Their self-concept in relation to their ability to succeed in university courses may be shaky, but they have chosen to teach, and this is something they must do. At the same time, they are confident and sure of their skills as electricians, carpenters, and automotive mechanics. How they see themselves and how they come to see themselves over the course of this transition is often transformative. Their self-concept is central to the process they undergo.

Although it is not often mentioned in the transformative learning literature, I see learning style as an important consideration in understanding how people experience transformation. I have long advocated for an expansion of the description of transformative learning that is open to an understanding of learning style (Cranton, 2006). I explore this more fully in Chapter 5.

Perspectives on Adult Learning

There are many patterns or systems of understanding adult learning. In their classic book, *The Profession and Practice of Adult Education: An Introduction*, Merriam and Brocket (1997) presented a philosophical classification system that included liberalism, progressivism, behaviorism, humanism, and radicalism. The oldest philosophy in Western society is liberal education, where the goal is to produce "intelligent, informed, cultured, and moral citizenry" (p. 33). In the mid-nineteenth century, progressivism emerged in response to industrialization. In this philosophy, more emphasis is placed on knowledge derived from science and rationality, and experience is seen as a source of learning. The behaviorists of the 1950s saw learning as a change in behavior that occurs as people respond to stimuli from the environment and are rewarded or punished. Knowledge is seen to be external to the self. Humanist philosophies came forward in reaction to behaviorism, although the roots of this way of thinking are much older. The humanists of the 1960s viewed learning as personal development through interpersonal relationships, which, in turn, contribute to the common good of humanity. The radical or critical philosophical framework of education came to the fore in the late 1960s and early 1970s through the work of Paulo Freire and Ivan Illich. The goal is social change through challenges to the current capitalist and democratic systems. Feminist theory has also contributed to the thinking of radical educators.

It may be helpful to think of there being at least two dimensions underlying the different perspectives on adult learning. The first dimension is the individual to social continuum. Some theorists and some practitioners prefer to focus on the individual's learning process, whereas others are more interested in social change and advocating for reform. Humanists tend to be interested in individual development and critical theorists in social reform. Transformative learning can be viewed from either perspective (Brookfield, 2000, 2012), and, indeed, this is a debate in the literature. Perhaps it need not be an either-or issue, but simply a preference as to where educators wish to spend their time and energy. Both individual and social perspectives are important, and obviously both exist, one within the other. We become individuals in a society.

The second dimension has to do with kinds of knowledge—the interests that drive the learning process and the type of knowledge that results from the learning. This is not a continuum, but rather a set of interrelated understandings of the world and ourselves within that world (i.e., the individual-social continuum exists within kinds of knowledge). It is helpful, in locating transformative learning within the larger arena of adult learning theory, to see how it is connected to the different kinds of knowledge with which educators work. Does a trades instructor have the potential to foster transformative learning? Does a literacy educator? A teacher of nursing? There are many ways of classifying knowledge, as anyone who has ventured into philosophy can attest. Here I use Habermas's (1971) original work. I choose this foundation as it is one Mezirow (1991) drew upon when he introduced his comprehensive transformative learning theory.

Technical Knowledge

The first kind of knowledge is *technical knowledge*, is that which allows us to manipulate and control the environment or to predict observable physical and social events and take appropriate actions. Empirical or natural scientific methodologies produce technically useful knowledge, the knowledge necessary for industry and production in modern society. In this paradigm, knowledge is established by reference to external reality, using the senses. There is an objective world made up of observable phenomena. The laws governing physical and social systems can be identified through science, and these systems are seen to operate independently of human perceptions. Habermas (1971) criticized instrumental rationality when it becomes such a pervasive ideology that we either believe all knowledge is instrumental or try to fit all knowledge into that category. In the Age of Enlightenment, the application of reason was seen as the way to solve the world's problems. As a result, empirical scientific methods were viewed as superior to subjective, qualitative, or spiritual ways of knowing. Only recently has modernism (the reign of logic) been criticized in the social sciences and education as not allowing a deeper, more open understanding of human interactions.

Mezirow (1991) defined *instrumental learning* as the acquisition of technical knowledge. Much of adult education practice has instrumental learning as a goal. Workplace programs often consist of training and retraining programs that focus on instrumental learning. Trades and technology programs contain both theoretical and practical, hands-on learning in concrete areas such as marine or automobile mechanics, silviculture, dental hygiene, and electronic communications. A good proportion of professional development for health professionals emphasizes new scientific information and techniques. However, problems arise when areas such as interpersonal relations and communications are treated as instrumental learning and forced into the training model.

Practical Knowledge

The second kind of knowledge is based on our need to understand each other through language. Habermas (1971) called this *practical* or *communicative knowledge*. Human beings have always been social creatures, instinctively forming groups, tribes, communities, cultures, and nations in order to satisfy their mutual needs. In order for people to survive together in groups and societies, they must communicate with and understand each other. There are no scientific laws governing these communications—when we communicate with others, we interpret what they say in our own way. This does not mean that communicative knowledge is entirely individual. All societies share and transmit social knowledge—that is, a code of commonly accepted beliefs and behavior. As a society we come to agree on how things should be and are in reference to standards and values, moral and political issues, educational and social systems, and government actions. Communicative knowledge is derived from shared interpretation and consensus and then often becomes reified. Habermas criticized communicative knowledge as being too dependent on subjective understanding. He argued that people may misinterpret the world around them based on distorted assumptions about themselves or society. We want social knowledge to be objective and concrete and therefore stop questioning the systems around us, unaware of the distortions that may exist in our assumptions.

It is fairly obvious that the acquisition of practical or communicative knowledge comprises a good deal of what people do in adult and higher education. Studies in psychology, sociology, politics, education, language, literature, fine arts, and history focus on communicative learning. Leadership training, interpersonal skills, teamwork, conflict resolution, communication skills, and the new emphasis on emotional intelligence illustrate the importance of communicative learning in workplace settings. In most places where people are working collaboratively in groups to share and interpret their experiences and construct new understandings, communicative learning is taking place.

Emancipatory Knowledge

The third kind of knowledge, which derives from a questioning of instrumental and communicative knowledge, Habermas (1971) called *emancipatory*. By nature, people are interested in self-knowledge, growth, development, and freedom. Gaining emancipatory knowledge is dependent on our abilities to be self-determining and self-reflective. Self-determination can be described as the capacity to be aware and critical both of ourselves and of our social and cultural context. Self-reflection involves being aware and critical of our subjective perceptions of knowledge and of the constraints of social knowledge. Emancipatory knowledge is gained through a process of critically questioning ourselves and the social systems within which we live. The philosophical foundation of emancipatory knowledge lies in critical theory. In this paradigm, instrumental and communicative knowledge are not rejected but are seen as limiting. If we do not question current scientific and social theories and accepted truths, we may never realize how we are constrained by their inevitable distortions and errors. Without the possibility of critical questioning of ourselves and our beliefs, such constraining knowledge can be accepted by entire cultures.

Emancipatory learning has been a goal of adult education through time and, to some extent, across cultures. In a history of adult education in Britain, Harrison (1961) stated that "it has been in the main regarded as a movement for freedom and liberation, both personal . . . and social" (p. xii). In North America, Lindeman (1926) described ideal adult education as cooperative, nonauthoritarian, informal, and a quest for the roots of our preconceptions. Freire (1970) saw his work in literacy education in South America as a "deepening awareness of both the sociocultural reality which shapes [learners'] lives and . . . their capacity to transform that reality through action upon it" (p. 27).

A careful reading of Mezirow's (1991) expression of the goal of adult education as transformative learning reveals how it is drawn from Habermas's (1971) idea of emancipatory knowledge and also reflects the thinking of earlier theorists:

> The goal of adult education is to help adult learners become more critically reflective, participate more fully and freely in rational discourse and action, and advance developmentally by moving toward meaning perspectives that are more inclusive, discriminating, permeable, and integrative of experience. (pp. 224–225)

There have been variations in wording and debates about the role of critical reflection and discourse in the process, but the essence of this statement has remained at the core of transformative learning theory.

Emancipatory learning occurs in informal and formal educational settings, including community development groups, self-help groups, professional development programs, literacy education, union education, and political and environmental movements, to name just a few. Perhaps more importantly, emancipatory learning can occur in any setting where learning occurs. A person acquiring a technical skill can gain new self-confidence and begin to see his or her place in the world in a new light. When I first learned Blackboard and WebCT (software platforms for online teaching), I acquired instrumental knowledge, but as a result I also revised my perspective on what good education is. In some of the great social change movements in adult education, such as the Antigonish Movement in Canada (MacKeracher, 2009), people obtained basic economic, literacy, and social skills, which provided them with the foundation for emancipatory learning.

Perspectives on Adult Learning: Integration

Now that I have taken apart the different kinds of learning in order to see what place transformative learning has, I would like to put them back together again before we proceed to the next chapters. I find it useful to categorize things in order to understand them, but I also find it limiting and fragmenting to leave these things in their categories.

Let us think about Steve's learning. I worked with Steve in a recent summer school program, and although I have changed information that might identify him, the story follows his journey. Steve is a marine mechanic in his late 40s. Steve has come to university to work on a certificate in adult education in hopes of finding a position teaching his trade. Steve's hands bear the marks of his years in his trade—they look swollen and stiff, and the black of engine grease seems worn into his skin. He dresses in jeans and a T-shirt, even though most of the other men in the group wear shorts during the hot summer days (our classroom has no air-conditioning). Steve is friendly, he smiles often, and he is quiet in class.

Steve is nervous about a good many things, as can be imagined. For this discussion's purposes, I am going to concentrate on just one of those things—his need to acquire a variety of technical computer skills. Steve had struggled through one online course, impeded by his poor keyboarding and his lack of familiarity with computers, where he had been learning to use e-mail and e-mail attachments. In our course, he decided to participate in a blog with a classmate. When a few others in the group offered to teach PowerPoint to those who were interested, Steve was enthusiastic about this opportunity as well. He was not sure how these skills would be useful in his future teaching career, but he felt they were things he should know.

Steve's acquisition of the technical skills required to participate in the blog and to create a PowerPoint presentation occur with a mixture of joy, anxiety, and, I sense, a feeling of being an imposter. What is he doing here? How do all of these things fit together? Should he be in a university course? How can he contribute to others' learning in the way his classmates are contributing to his? It would be impossible, I think, to separate Steve's instrumental learning from his communicative learning. As he participates in the blog, the skills he learns are simultaneously applied to his dialogue with his peers and with me. It is not that he learns something and then uses it later in a different way—the two occur together. To learn PowerPoint, we are all together in a computer lab, and three of the course members lead the learning. I am participating as a learner, but I notice how it is going with Steve and other newcomers to this technology. Again, the technical skill is learned and simultaneously used to create something that communicates with others. Steve is excited; he shares his work with those near him, and he looks around laughing.

I can see the two strands—instrumental and communicative learning—but I cannot see how they could be separated. And what of the emancipatory learning? Steve questioned his assumptions about who he was and what he was capable of doing and revised his self-perceptions in such a way that they were more open and better justified. (I also had the opportunity to read his autobiography and his reflections on the course, which supported my observations of his learning.) He became free of some fairly overwhelming constraints stemming from his past habits of mind. Of course, I cannot attribute all of this to his participating in a blog or learning PowerPoint, but neither can I separate it from that learning. In his final reflection and self-evaluation, Steve said that "everything came together," and he saw how he "could be a teacher." Things were no longer "little pieces"; rather, "the whole made sense." In this way, meaningful learning integrates instrumental and communicative knowledge, and emancipatory learning occurs when that knowledge changes a person's perspective of himself and the world.

Steve's story is not representative, of course, of all learning experiences, though I see it often enough to be sure that it is not unique either. Still, there are times when people go along acquiring large amounts of instrumental or communicative knowledge before the pieces come together, and there are many occasions when emancipatory learning does not occur. As Mezirow (2000) said, learning can also be the acquisition of new knowledge or elaboration on existing knowledge without calling into question any previously held assumptions or beliefs. However, as educators I think we should always be conscious of the potential of those moments when the acquisition of new knowledge can move into the realm of emancipation. In order to do this, we need to be aware of the wholeness of learning. As useful as it would appear on the surface to be able to say that "this is going to be transformative learning" and "this cannot be transformative," I think we would do ourselves a disservice to try to define types of learning out of context. We know that transformative learning involves a deep shift in perspective and that it leads to a way of seeing the world that is more open. But we cannot say what kind of a learning experience will promote this shift in perspective in any person or any context.

Summary

Transformative learning theory has taken a central place in the adult education, higher education, and professional education literature. There are conferences and a journal dedicated to transformative learning; the offerings in both the journal and the conference confirm the degree to which the interest in transformative learning has spread beyond adult education. In this chapter, I have situated transformative learning within the broader field in two ways. First, I reviewed some of the characteristics that are used to characterize adult learning—the voluntary and collaborative nature of adult learning, adults' preference for self-direction, the importance of meeting practical needs, the role of adults' experiences in their learning, the relevance of self-concept, and the emphasis on learning styles. Not all of these characteristics are unique to adult education; they are relevant to students in higher education, younger learners, professionals, and leaders and staff in organizations. In this chapter, I explored how each of these qualities is an attribute of transformative learning.

Second, I looked at different perspectives on learning, starting with a brief overview of philosophies of learning. I think there are at least two dimensions underlying the way we see learning—the individual-social continuum and the kinds of knowledge in which we are interested. I discussed this latter dimension in more depth using Habermas's three types of knowledge (from which Mezirow found a basis for transformative learning theory). Technical knowledge is the cause-and-effect, objective, scientific knowledge that allows us to control and manipulate our environment. Practical or communicative knowledge is the knowledge of ourselves, others, and our social world. Emancipatory knowledge is that which frees us from personal and social constraints and leads to awareness and development. It is emancipatory learning, which is based on the critical examination of instrumental and communicative knowledge, that is transformative.

To conclude this chapter, I argued that any classification system is limiting and proposed that we often cannot separate kinds of learning. I illustrated this with the story of Steve, whose acquisition of instrumental and communicative knowledge occurred simultaneously with his emancipatory learning. Transformative learning is a subset of how adults learn in a variety of contexts, but not all learning is transformative and it does not occur separately from other kinds of learning. It is when instrumental and communicative learning leads us to question our previously held views about ourselves and the world around us that the potential for transformative learning exists.

2

THE ORIGINS OF
TRANSFORMATIVE
LEARNING THEORY

Throughout their lifetimes, people make meaning out of their experiences. They build a way of seeing the world; settle on a way of interpreting what happens to them; and develop the accompanying values, beliefs, and assumptions that determine their behavior. Much of this framework is uncritically absorbed from family, community, and culture. People do not stop to question everything that happens to them or everything they see and hear—they generally believe their friends, accept media interpretations of events, and follow the principles that have guided them so far. People have a set of expectations about the world that are based on formative childhood experiences, and those expectations continue to act as a filter for understanding life.

When something unexpected happens, when a person encounters something that does not fit with his or her expectations of how things should be based on past experience, the choices are to reject the unexpected or to question the expectation. When people critically examine their habitual expectations, revise them, and act on the revised point of view, transformative learning occurs. Transformative learning leads to perspectives that are more inclusive, discriminating, and integrative of experience (Mezirow, 2000).

In this chapter, I briefly outline how transformative learning theory developed from 1975 to the present and then turn to a full description of the theory. I use Mezirow's work as the foundation for the description in this chapter, as it was his research, writing, and theory development that provides the foundations for our current thinking about and applications of transformative learning theory.

15

Development of Transformative Learning Theory

When this chapter was drafted, it had been 40 years since Jack Mezirow introduced the term *perspective transformation* to the literature. He passed away in the fall of 2014, just before the 40th anniversary of his initial study. Mezirow responded to his wife Edee's experience in returning to school and embarked on a study of 83 women returning to college in 12 different reentry programs. Mezirow (1978, 1991) described a process of personal perspective transformation that included 10 phases:

1. Experiencing a disorienting dilemma
2. Undergoing self-examination
3. Conducting a critical assessment of internalized assumptions and feeling a sense of alienation from traditional social expectations
4. Relating discontent to the similar experiences of others—recognizing that the problem is shared
5. Exploring options for new ways of acting
6. Building competence and self-confidence in new roles
7. Planning a course of action
8. Acquiring the knowledge and skills for implementing a new course of action
9. Trying out new roles and assessing them
10. Reintegrating into society with the new perspective (adapted from Mezirow, 1991, pp. 168–169)

It is interesting to note that six of the phases have to do with preparation for and implementation of new, revised perspectives. In more recent years, the emphasis has been much more on encountering the disorienting event and critically questioning or responding to the assumptions and expectations that make it disorienting.

The results of Mezirow's research led him to outline a theory of adult development that he called perspective transformation—"a structural reorganization in the way that a person looks at himself and his relationships" (Mezirow, 1975, p. 162).

In 1981, Mezirow drew on Habermas's (1971) three kinds of learning (see Chapter 1) in order to construct what he termed a *critical theory of adult learning and education*. Mezirow equated emancipatory action with perspective transformation in this writing. At that time, he was interested in "psycho-cultural assumptions" (Mezirow, 1981, p. 6)—the way in which a person's past constrains perceptions of the self and relationships with others.

In 1985, Mezirow elaborated on his concept of perspective transformation and related it to self-directed learning, another concept that had been introduced by Knowles (1975) in his book *Self-Directed Learning.* He did not follow the problem-solving, instructional design approach to self-directed learning as proposed by Knowles. Instead, Mezirow (1985) described learning as a process of making assumptions explicit, contextualizing them, validating them, and acting on them. Education was the process of fostering this effort, and self-directedness was the ability to understand our own experiences. He described a self-directed learner as one who participates freely in dialogue in order to test perspectives against those of others and modify them accordingly (Mezirow, 1985). In other words, a self-directed learner was one who engaged in transformative learning. At that time, too, *meaning perspectives* were defined as the structure or web of cultural and psychological assumptions and *meaning schemes* functioned as the rules and expectations that govern our lives (Mezirow, 1985).

Mezirow's use of Habermas's work was criticized as being inaccurate, and, in response, he suggested that emancipatory learning was not a separate domain but rather applicable to both instrumental and communicative learning (Mezirow, 1989). In 1990, he edited *Fostering Critical Reflection in Adulthood,* in which he gathered together several authors' diverse perspectives on how critical reflection and hence transformative learning could be fostered (Mezirow, 1990). However his 1991 book, *Transformative Dimensions of Adult Learning,* brought the theory to the forefront of the adult education literature. This work was criticized for not including issues to do with social action, power, and cultural context. It was also judged as being too rational, thereby ignoring the role of intuitions, symbols, and images in learning. Mezirow invited and encouraged critiques of his work, hoping that the theory would continue to evolve within the community of educators interested in transformative learning. However, he maintained his stance that transformation was a cognitive, rational process: "Transformative learning is understood as a uniquely adult form of metacognitive reasoning. Reasoning is the process of advancing and assessing reasons, especially those that provide arguments supporting beliefs resulting in decisions to act. Beliefs are justified when they are based on good reasons" (Mezirow, 2003b, p. 58).

In 2000, Mezirow edited *Learning as Transformation: Critical Perspectives on a Theory in Progress,* based in part on papers presented at the first International Transformative Learning Conference, held in 1998 at Teachers College, Columbia University. In his own chapter in that volume, Mezirow acknowledged the importance of the affective, emotional, and social context aspects of transformative learning. He also agreed that there were "asymmetrical power relationships" (p. 28) in the learning process. Other chapters presented diverse points of view on transformative learning such as Daloz's (2000) developmental approach and Belenky and Stanton's (2000) concept of connected knowing. I further discuss how Mezirow's theory was expanded and elaborated on in Chapter 3.

Around this same time, Mezirow (2000, 2003a) introduced some new terminology—*habits of mind* and *points of view*. He earlier described a frame of reference as the web of assumptions and expectations through which we filter the way we see the world. A frame of reference has two dimensions—a habit of mind and the resulting points of view. Habits of mind are the broad predispositions that we use to interpret experience. A habit of mind is expressed as a point of view. A point of view is a cluster of meaning schemes, and meaning schemes are habitual, implicit rules for interpreting experiences.

Baumgartner (2012) has provided an excellent review of Mezirow's work from 1975 until 2012, including the beginning of the theory in the late 1970s, the refinement of the theory in the 1980s, the revision of the theory in the 1990s, and the "theory in progress" in the 2000s.

Overview of Transformative Learning Theory

Transformative learning theory is based on constructivist assumptions. In other words, meaning is seen to exist within ourselves, not in external forms. We develop or construct personal meaning from our experience and validate it through interaction and communication with others. What we make of the world is a result of our perceptions of our experiences. If we were to claim the existence of absolute truths or universal constructs that are independent of our knowledge of them, the goal of learning would be to discover the right answers rather than to contemplate our perspectives on the world. Transformative learning is a process of examining, questioning, validating, and revising our perspectives. In 2003, Mezirow wrote,

> Transformative learning is learning that transforms problematic frames of reference—sets of fixed assumptions and expectations (habits of mind, meaning perspectives, mindsets)—to make them more inclusive, discriminating, open, reflective, and emotionally able to change. Such frames of reference are better than others because they are more likely to generate beliefs and opinions that will prove more true or justified to guide action. (Mezirow, 2003b, pp. 58–59)

Our experiences are filtered through our meaning perspectives or habits of mind, which include uncritically assimilated ways of knowing, believing, and feeling. They include distortions, prejudices, stereotypes, and simply unquestioned or unexamined beliefs. Maintaining a meaning perspective is safe.

Learning occurs when an individual encounters an alternative perspective that calls prior habits of mind into question. Mezirow originally saw this as a single, dramatic event—a disorienting dilemma—but he and others (Mezirow, 2000; E. W. Taylor, 2000) have since acknowledged that it could also be a gradual cumulative process. Mezirow (2000) described transformative learning that is stimulated by a dramatic event as epochal and that which is more gradual as incremental. Dirkx (2000) proposed that transformative learning is more often a process of everyday occurrences than it is a so-called burning bush phenomenon.

If a person responds to an alternative habit of mind by reconsidering and revising prior belief systems, the learning becomes transformative. As Mezirow (1991) put it, "Reflective learning becomes transformative whenever assumptions or premises are found to be distorting, inauthentic, or otherwise invalid" (p. 6).

In all of Mezirow's writing, discourse is central to transformative learning. He defined *discourse* as dialogue involving the assessment of beliefs, feelings, and values (Mezirow, 2003b, p. 59). Under ideal conditions (which cannot be established completely), participants in discourse will:

- Have accurate and complete information
- Be free from coercion and distorting self-perception
- Be able to weigh evidence and assess arguments objectively
- Be open to alternative perspectives
- Be able to reflect critically on presuppositions and their consequences
- Have equal opportunity to participate
- Be able to accept an informed, objective consensus as valid (Mezirow, 1991, p. 78)

Types of Habits of Mind

Mezirow (1991) originally distinguished among three kinds of meaning perspectives—epistemic, sociolinguistic, and psychological—but he went on to expand this to include six habits of mind (Mezirow, 2000). To the original three kinds of meaning perspectives he added moral-ethical, philosophical, and aesthetic habits of mind. He did not see these categories as independent, but rather as overlapping and influencing each other. A habit of mind is a way of seeing the world based on our background, experience, culture, and personality. Because all of our habits of mind are determined by our personal stories, it is reasonable to expect that they are interrelated.

Epistemic habits of mind are those related to knowledge and the way we acquire and use knowledge. For example, Coke, Benson, and Hayes (2015) described the transition from graduate student to professor as a transformative experience based on revisions in knowledge about teaching and learning in the person's role as English language arts instructor. For more than two decades, I had deeply held convictions about the nature of teaching as involving face-to-face communication. When Steve (in Chapter 1) learned how to use PowerPoint, it was not only a technical skill that he acquired, but also a revision to his epistemic assumptions about teaching—his knowledge about teaching.

Epistemic habits of mind are also about the way we learn—learning styles and preferences. Whether a person thinks globally or in detail, concretely or abstractly, or in an organized or intuitive way will involve epistemic perspectives that are influenced by those preferences. We do not easily change the way we learn. These preferences are very much about who we are as human beings; they are long-held and deeply valued ways of seeing ourselves. For me to move away from my analytical approach to understanding theory, for example, seems almost impossible, and I only catch glimpses of how it might be to approach learning in different ways.

Sociolinguistic habits of mind are based on social norms, cultural expectations, and the way we use language. Media images of war and violence form our perceptions of violence. Growing up in a culture in which women's roles are clearly defined as submissive shape our habits of mind about how women should behave. For example, Mejiuni (2012) conducted a comprehensive study of the roles of women in Nigeria and the influence of power and violence on their lives; through sociolinguistic habits of mind, women are expected to be caring, nurturing, and to act as peacekeepers, a view reinforced by religious leaders. Mejiuni argued that violence against women is a consequence of the unequal power relations between women and men.

In a panel presentation at the Adult Educational Research Conference, Brookfield, Sheared, Johnson-Bailey, and Colin (2005) probed the dominant, mainstream perspectives on race through a sharing of experiences and stories. The constructs are deep and unconsciously absorbed. White adult educators cannot enter the world of their colleagues of color and even attempting to do so can paradoxically emphasize their privilege. It is no simple matter to bring our sociolinguistic habits of mind to the forefront of consciousness and consider them in a way that has the potential to lead to transformation.

Psychological habits of mind have to do with how people see themselves—their self-concept, needs, inhibitions, anxieties, and fears. Feeling unloved as a child could lead to feeling unworthy as an adult. Someone whose parents had very high expectations of achievement in school may develop a perspective that includes great motivation to achieve or possibly a sense of guilt about never being able to achieve enough. The sources of psychological habits of mind are often buried in childhood experiences, including trauma, and may not be easily accessible to the conscious self.

Personality traits also comprise a facet of our psychological habits of mind (see Chapter 5). Whether we prefer to make judgments using thinking or feeling, whether we have an introverted or extraverted attitude toward the world, and whether we perceive the world through our senses or through our intuition act as filters in how we see the world.

Moral-ethical habits of mind incorporate conscience and morality. How people determine good and evil, how they act on their views of goodness, and the extent to which they see themselves as responsible for advocating for justice in the world create a perspective for making meaning out of the world. People donate time and money to charitable organizations, protest against war, boycott products and services, and stop to help a neighbor based on moral-ethical habits of mind.

Brookfield (2005), in his discussion of Habermas's view of social evolution, explained that "the development of morality is indicated by people's ability to detach themselves from everyday thinking and decide (after participating in discussions with others about the ethical justifications of various approaches to situations) how to act in ways that are not ideologically predetermined" (p. 257). Individuals can develop a moral consciousness that is of a higher stage than that which is embodied in the institutions of society.

Philosophical habits of mind can be based on a transcendental worldview, philosophy, or religious doctrine. Most religious systems contain a complex web of values, beliefs, guides to behavior, and rules for living. The acceptance of a particular religious system, whether it is consciously chosen or assimilated from family, creates a powerful meaning perspective. Everything from style of dress to political views may be dictated. Philosophical habits of mind based on a worldview are similarly complex. A neighbor of mine, for example, subscribes to a "social credit" worldview that is described as a "whole orientation to civilization," including the social, political, and economic aspects of living—it calls for a redistribution of wealth, radically different views of employment, the end of capitalism, and so forth.

Aesthetic habits of mind include our values, attitudes, tastes, judgments, and standards about beauty. Aesthetic habits of mind are, in large part, sociolinguistic habits of mind; that is, they are determined by the social norms of the community and culture. Of course, it is possible to be a part of a culture and not hold the same standards about beauty, just as it is possible to reject other subsets of cultural expectations and remain within that culture.

Aesthetic habits of mind may have an even broader meaning. Marcuse (1978), who believed we cannot rely only on our reason, proposed that powerful aesthetic experiences through art, music, and fiction had the potential to help people detach themselves from their everyday world and see a fundamentally different point of view. Lawrence (2012) described how art breaks us out of the boundaries that constrain us. Both for individuals and communities, she suggested that creating and viewing art allows us to "surface knowledge that was always present but outside of our conscious awareness" (p. 473).

Each of these six kinds of habits of mind is interdependent and interrelated. As helpful as it is to think about different kinds of perspectives, it is just as important to see the interconnections. My way of seeing myself (psychological habit of mind) is influenced by my cultural background (sociolinguistic habit of mind). By growing up in an isolated and poor community that did not value education (sociolinguistic habit of mind), I ended up with great gaps in my knowledge (epistemic habit of mind). Moral-ethical and aesthetic habits of mind are obviously deeply influenced by sociolinguistic, psychological, and epistemic factors. If, for example, I know little about classical music or art (epistemic perspective), my tastes and standards about beauty (aesthetic perspective) will be very different from those of a person well informed in the arts. Philosophical habits of mind may provide an umbrella for many other of our perspectives.

Unquestioned Habits of Mind

The way we see the world is a product of our knowledge about the world, our cultural background and language, our psychological nature, our moral and ethical views, the religious doctrine or worldview to which we subscribe, and the way we see beauty. Each perspective is made up of interwoven beliefs, values, feelings, and assumptions that together create the lens through which we see the world and form the basis for our actions in the world. That I choose to rescue animals whereas someone else chooses to kill them reflects our different points of view. That someone protests against an American-led war on Iraq whereas someone else acts as a suicide bomber illustrates opposing worldviews.

Habits of mind are unexamined. They create limitations and form boxes of which we are unconscious and cannot, therefore, get beyond. In his 1991 book, Mezirow referred to these as distorted meaning perspectives, but the term *distorted* raises questions. If we adhere to a realistic view of the world, then distorted assumptions might be helpful in understanding our stance in relation to that world. However, if we hold a constructivist worldview, we are left with several questions. Who, for example, has the privilege of deciding which perspectives are distorted? If a student finds her perspective to be just fine, can a teacher imply that it is distorted? If a whole community or culture accepts a certain point of view (e.g, polygamy is evil, war is necessary), does that mean the view is not distorted? Yet we also do not want to fall into the trap of saying that all opinions and beliefs are equally good and acceptable. It seems that one way through this dilemma is to refer to unquestioned or unexamined rather than distorted habits of mind. This also allows the possibility that habits of mind do not necessarily need to be abandoned once examined.

Adult developmental theorists give us some help in understanding the characteristics of unquestioned habits of mind. The stage theories of development tend to show a progression of development from simplistic black-and-white perceptions of the world through to complex relativistic perceptions. The classic theories of adult development all reflect this progression: Perry's (1970) well-known approach to cognitive development; King and Kitchener's (1994) work on reflective judgment; and Belenky, Clinchy, Goldberger, and Tarule's (1986) work on women's ways of knowing. For example, King and Kitchener's (1994) model of reflective judgment contained the following seven stages:

1. Beliefs need no justification; what is believed is true.
2. Knowledge is absolutely certain but may not be immediately available.
3. Knowledge is absolutely certain or temporarily uncertain.
4. Knowledge is idiosyncratic, and some information may be in error or lost; therefore, one cannot know with certainty.
5. Knowledge is contextual and subjective; it is available through interpretation.
6. Knowledge is constructed by each person and is based on the evaluation of evidence and argument.
7. Knowledge is the product of rational inquiry, which is fallible.

More recently, K. Taylor and Elias (2012) based their discussion of a developmental perspective on Kegan's (2000) model of transformations of consciousness. Kegan was interested in not so much what we know but how we know, the "form" of the learning rather than the content. His model moved from the socialized self to beyond socialization (the self-authorizing self) and finally to self-transforming (a stage that few individuals reach).

Mark Tennant has a long history of writing about adult development in relation to transformative learning. His most recent book (Tennant, 2012) took an interesting perspective that is somewhat related to Kegan's work. He analyzed the different concepts of self and related each to the transformative learning process. The *authentic self* implies that there "is an essence that is you . . . the essential self" (p. 17), which may be biologically determined or learned but is resistant to change. The *autonomous self* is "characterized by agency, choice, reflection, and rationality" (p. 35). The *repressed self* takes into account the unconscious dimension. Tennant relied on Freud (1963) for this discussion, but Jung (1971) may be more relevant as his conceptualization included individuation, which is akin to transformative learning. The *socially constructed self* is developed through interactions with others. Finally the *storied self* explains how individuals use storytelling and narrative to come to an understanding of the self.

Mezirow (1991) described sociolinguistic habits of mind as being very difficult to articulate and question. As can be seen in the developmental approaches of K. Taylor and Elias, Kegan, and Tennant, we are deeply embedded in our social world and cannot easily stand outside of it to look at its norms and expectations. Habermas (1984) wrote of a system world. Systems, such as a monetary system that has evolved from ownership and the exchange of possessions, have been removed from the realm of individual control. They are no longer questioned or seen as questionable. Rarely do people debate the value of having a legal system, or the necessity of using money as a means of exchange of property, or whether educational institutions should exist. We tend to be unaware of the social codes in which power and privilege are distributed.

When critical theorists encourage us to deconstruct commonly held points of view and when postmodernists "trouble" or "complicate" beliefs, they are trying to prod these deeply embedded habits of mind.

In his early, comprehensive presentation of his theory, Mezirow (1991) discussed several ways in which habits of mind become seemingly unquestionable:

- Language-based assumptions are especially insidious, as we need to use language itself to question. Through labeling, we attach the characteristics of the label to the person or thing we have labeled; when that label is uncritically assimilated, it is hard to call it into question.
- We operate with selective perception. We cannot see and hear everything, so we choose to pay attention to some things and ignore others. It is easier to pay attention to that with which we already agree.
- Freire's (1970) levels of consciousness remind us that different thoughts are easier at different times. For example, there are times when people are preoccupied with survival needs, internalize the values of their oppressors, or are impressed with populist leaders. Critical examination of habits of mind is unlikely to occur under those conditions.
- People may have constrained visions of humanity. They see humanity as flawed; no amount of reason, effort, or action will make a difference (students are lazy and not motivated, workers do not care about their jobs, the public is stupid and naïve).

Our unquestioned psychological beliefs and assumptions may cause us pain because they are inconsistent with how we prefer to see ourselves as adults. They can be defense mechanisms originating in childhood trauma, mechanisms that are dysfunctional in adulthood. Those theorists who have taken a depth psychology approach to transformative learning (e.g., Dirkx, 2012) have emphasized the power of the unconscious in shaping how we see ourselves. M. Watkins (2000) described the unconscious as being made up of clusters of psychic energy or different selves that inform the conscious self. By definition, the *unconscious* is unexamined and unquestioned. Bringing the unconscious into consciousness is part of what Dirkx (2001a) termed *soul work*.

In today's society, with the media attention given to physical, sexual, and psychological abuse, we are well aware of the powerful and lifelong impact such tragic experiences can have on people's lives. In these cases, Mezirow's (1991) original term *distorted assumptions* seems reasonable. It is most often the role of counselors and therapists more so than the role of adult educators to help individuals work through these perspectives.

The source of our unexamined psychological habits of mind can also be more prosaic. Simple childhood experiences that would not necessarily be labeled as traumatic can have a profound impact on self-perception. For example, I think of my well-meaning grandmother who told me that my legs were "big," and therefore she would pay me 25 cents not to wear shorts. To this day, I am uncomfortable in shorts or short skirts and rarely wear them.

And, of course, past educational experiences, such as childhood school failure and criticism by teachers or peers, can contribute to people's perceptions of themselves as learners. Individuals who see themselves as incompetent learners, unable to write or study or incapable of critical thinking, for example, can likely connect their self-concept to earlier learning experiences.

Types of Reflection

Reflection is a key concept in transformative learning theory. In adult education generally, reflective thinking is a goal of learning. This notion can be traced to Dewey (1933), who defined *reflection* as "active, persistent and careful consideration of any belief or supposed form of knowledge in the light of the grounds that support it and the further conclusion to which it tends" (p. 9). Current definitions of *reflection* do not differ substantially from Dewey's understanding. Reflection is still seen as a process of reconsidering experience through reason and reinterpreting and generalizing the experience to form mental structures (Fenwick, 1998; Mezirow, 2003b).

Mezirow has always maintained that critical reflection is central to transformative learning. In 2003, he suggested that two distinctively adult learning capabilities are required: the development of a capacity to be critically self-reflective (Kegan, 2000) and to exercise reflective judgment (King & Kitchener, 1994). Mezirow (2003b) wrote, "These adult capabilities are indispensable for fully understanding the meaning of our experience and effective rational adult reasoning in critical discourse and communicative learning" (p. 60). Transformative learning requires critical reflection from this perspective.

Although Mezirow no longer emphasized distinctions among content, process, and premise reflection (Mezirow, 1991), I continue to find it useful in my practice and thinking about critical reflection, so I include it here.

Content reflection is an examination of the content or description of a problem. It is the equivalent of asking, "What is happening here? What is the problem?" If a learner of automobile mechanics encounters a new piece of equipment for diagnosing fuel injection problems, he or she might ask, "What is this? What does it do? What use might I make of it?" The student could try to determine the characteristics of the equipment, observe someone else using it, or read the manual that came with it. This would form content reflection on a problem related to instrumental knowledge.

In another domain of knowledge, a student returning to an adult education center to obtain her high school equivalency might feel uncomfortable and out of place. She might ask, "What is happening here? What am I feeling?" She could reflect on her reactions to the situation to try to determine if she is worried about her study skills, feeling socially out of place, or fearful of not being able to succeed. This could be the beginning of a reflective process that would lead to emancipatory learning.

Process reflection involves checking on the problem-solving strategies that are being used. It is asking "How did this come to be?" Let us say that the student of mechanics was unable to immediately identify and use the new piece of equipment. He or she might stop and review the process used so far and ask, "Did I miss something? Do I not understand the manual? Did I misinterpret what my teachers said?" The learner is reflecting on the process of understanding the problem. Similarly, the individual who returns to school and questions her self-perception might ask, "How have I ended up feeling this way? Do I understand myself? Am I overlooking something? How is it that I am unable to adapt?"

Premise reflection takes place when the problem itself is questioned. Reflection takes the form of "Why is this important to me? Why do I care about this in the first place? What difference does this make? Why is this a problem anyway?" It is an examination of the premise or basis of the problem. The student of mechanics could ask, "Why do I need to operate this equipment? Am I just doing this because someone told me to, or is it really important? Is this just a promotion by the manufacturer? Do I need this?" The learner returning to complete her high school equivalency could ask, "Why am I making this into a problem? Isn't it natural to feel anxious?"

It is premise reflection that has the potential to lead people to the transformation of a habit of mind. Mezirow (1991, 2000) distinguished between transformative learning that involves the revision of a specific assumption or belief and transformative learning that incorporates the revision of a more complex, wider perspective. Content and process reflection may lead to the transformation of a specific belief, but it is premise reflection that engages learners in seeing themselves and the world in a different way. With premise reflection the student of mechanics could come to see fundamental aspects of the trade differently—how new equipment is introduced and by whom and for what reasons. And with premise reflection, the high school returnee could revise her entire way of reacting to new situations.

In my practice, I find asking reflective questions of these types very useful as do my students, who are also adult educators. I include more about critical questioning in Chapter 8 and also in my other writings (e.g., see Cranton, 2003). For our purposes here, I include several different forms that content, process, and premise reflection questions might take, depending on the nature of the habit of mind and the kind of knowledge. Table 2.1 includes questions for each of the types of habits of mind, and Table 2.2 contains question formats for Habermas's knowledge domains.

Summary

In the 40 years since Mezirow studied the experiences of women returning to college, transformative learning theory has developed from a 10-step transition model to a complex and comprehensive theory of adult learning. Although Mezirow remained constant in his view that transformation occurs through rational critical self-reflection and discourse, others in the field have elaborated on the ways in which it may occur.

Transformative learning is defined as the process by which people examine problematic frames of reference to make them more inclusive, discriminating, open, reflective, and emotionally able to change. It can be provoked by a single event—a disorienting dilemma—or it can take place gradually and cumulatively over time. Discourse is central to the process. We need to

TABLE 2.1
Reflective Questions for Habits of Mind

Reflection	Habit of Mind		
	Psychological	Sociolinguistic	Epistemic
Content	What do I believe about myself?	What are the social norms?	What knowledge do I have?
Process	How have I come to have this perception of myself?	How have these social norms been influential?	How did I obtain this knowledge?
Premise	Why should I question this perception?	Why are these norms important?	Why do I need or not need this knowledge?
	Moral-ethical	Philosophical	Aesthetic
Content	What are my values?	What is my worldview?	What do I find beautiful?
Process	How have my values formed?	How have I come to hold this worldview?	How have my views of beauty been shaped?
Premise	Why are my values important?	Why do I stay with this worldview?	Why do I care about beauty?

TABLE 2.2
Reflective Questions for Kinds of Knowledge

Reflection	Knowledge		
	Instrumental	Communicative	Emancipatory
Content	What are the facts?	What do others say about this issue?	What are my assumptions?
Process	How do I know this is true?	How did I integrate others' points of view?	How do I know my assumptions are valid?
Premise	Why is this knowledge important to me?	Why should I believe in this conclusion?	Why should I revise or not revise my perspective?

engage in conversation with others in order to better consider alternative perspectives and determine their validity.

Frames of reference are made up of habits of mind (the broad predispositions that we use to interpret experience) and points of view (a cluster of habitual, implicit assumptions we use to interpret experience). A habit of mind is expressed as a point of view. If, for example, a person has a habit of mind that predisposes her to admire a strong work ethic, this may be expressed as a point of view in which she is critical of individuals who fraudulently collect unemployment benefits from the government.

Habits of mind may be of different types. Mezirow named six overlapping and interrelated habits of mind: epistemic, to do with knowledge and the way we acquire knowledge; sociolinguistic, based on social norms and the way language is used; psychological, to do with how people see themselves; moral-ethical, related to conscience and morality; philosophical, based on worldview or religious doctrine; and aesthetic, including our standards about beauty.

Habits of mind are uncritically absorbed from our families, community, and culture. They tend to remain unquestioned unless we encounter an alternative perspective that we cannot ignore. Unquestioned habits of mind may be a product of cognitive development, strong societal values, and personal experiences or traumas in childhood.

In Mezirow's view, critical reflection and critical self-reflection are central to transformative learning. In his 1991 book, he delineated three kinds of reflection: content, process, and premise. Content and process reflection (asking, "What is the problem?" and "How did this come to be a problem?") may lead to transformation of specific assumptions and beliefs. Premise reflection—challenging the very basis of the problem or issue—has the potential to promote transformation of habits of mind, the web of assumptions and beliefs that acts as a lens through which we see ourselves and the world around us.

3

TRANSFORMATIVE
LEARNING THEORY AS AN
INTEGRATED PERSPECTIVE

In 2000, Mezirow declared that transformative learning was a theory in progress by using this phrase in the subtitle of his edited book (*Learning as Transformation: Critical Perspectives on a Theory in Progress*), a book that was based on the presentations at the first International Transformative Learning Conference in 1998. This perspective has continued to be valued in the biannual transformative learning conferences and in the *Journal of Transformative Education* (published since 2003).

The earliest critics of transformative learning theory focused on Mezirow's failure to address social change and his selective interpretation of Habermas's work (Collard & Law, 1989), his neglect of power issues (Hart, 1990), his disregard for the cultural context of learning (M. C. Clark & Wilson, 1991), and his overemphasis on rational thought (Dirkx, 1997). These issues continue to be mentioned in most reviews of the literature on transformative learning. Since 2000, several scholars have focused on categorizing the different approaches to transformative learning theory. Baumgartner (2001) used Dirkx's (1998) four-lens approach to understanding the directions in which transformative learning theory has moved. The first lens has Freire's (1970) perspective as its foundation; that is, transformative learning's goal is liberation from oppression, and its orientation is social justice. The second lens is Mezirow's (2000) concentration on rational thought and reflection as central to a process of responding to a disorienting dilemma, questioning and revising assumptions, engaging in discourse, and acting on a new perspective (see Chapter 2). The third lens is a developmental approach to transformative learning (Daloz, 1999). Here the process is intuitive, holistic, and contextually based; it is a transitional journey that takes place within a social environment. And finally, the fourth lens through which transformative learning can be viewed is one in which learning is linked to spirituality (Dirkx, 2001b; Tis-dell & Tolliver, 2001). Dirkx described transformative learning as soul work; other writers have linked it to specific practices such as Buddhist meditation (Robinson, 2004) and yoga (Cohen, 2003).

E. W. Taylor (2008) identified several "alternative conceptions" of trans-formative learning: a psychoanalytical view (a process of individuation from a Jungian perspective), a psychodevelopmental view (learning across the life-span), a social-emancipatory view (where the oppressed develop a critical consciousness), a neurobiological view (which describes changes in the brain's structure during the learning process), a cultural-spiritual view (a culturally relevant and spiritually grounded approach), a race-centric view (which puts people of African descent at the center of the transformative process), and a planetary view (where transformative learning takes into account the whole system beyond the individual—interconnections among the universe, the natural environment, and the personal world).

This type of fragmentation is fairly typical in the development of a new theory, but the time has come to work toward integration rather than further fragmentation. In this chapter, I review the various threads of transforma-tive learning and explore the integration of these threads. I first describe the introduction of connected and relational learning into the theory, and then I provide some thoughts on transformative learning in relation to social change. These perspectives stretch the basic rationalistic views of Mezirow's theory and open the door for alternative ways of understanding transformative learning, yet they rely primarily on reflection to mediate the learning processes and, in this sense, are an extension of the emphasis on critical reflection described in Chapter 2. Here I discuss the application of transformative learning theory to groups and organizations and review how transformative learning can be seen as an approach to worldviews on globali-zation and environmentalism. I then turn to a description of the extrarational approach, which represents a fundamental challenge to critical reflection as a way of knowing by suggesting that transformative learning is mediated by unconscious processes beyond the level of rational and conscious awareness. I explore how these various strands of transformative learning can exist as an integrated theory of transformative learning. Finally, I summarize some of the research on transformative learning by drawing on E. W. Taylor and Snyder's (2012) review of that literature.

Connected Knowing

It is not just in regard to transformative learning theory that there has been considerable debate about whether learning is connected and relational or independent and autonomous (e.g., MacKeracher, 2004). Traditional learning theory focuses on how an individual person learns, and although the context of the learning may be considered, it is generally about that person, not that person learning in and from relationships with others. This sounds odd, given the emphasis on groups and interactive methods in education, but learning has long been seen as an individual process even though discussion and group work may be used to achieve learning. Perhaps the roots of this assumption lie in behaviorism, with its emphasis on the individual organism, or perhaps they lie in the models of assessment that drive educational systems. Intelligence and aptitude are always measured individually, and scoring systems are based on comparison and competition among individuals. Evaluation of learning is based on individual performance in education from the first grade through to doctoral studies.

Western society values individualism. Every aspect of our lives is influenced by this value, including how we think about learning (Brookfield, 2005). It should not be too big a surprise that we respect autonomous, independent learning. Since Gardner (Gardner, Kornhaber, & Wake, 1996) introduced multiple intelligences, one of which is interpersonal intelligence, and Goleman (2011) brought the concept of emotional intelligence to our attention, there has been a change in our collective perspective. In training programs and workplace education, more emphasis is placed on how people learn to work together. But still, this is primarily about how an individual person learns to work with others, not learn in relation to others.

Some feminist writers and theorists interested in gender differences in learning (English & Irving, 2012) have suggested that women have been ignored in the literature on transformative learning. Hayes and Flannery (2000) emphasized relational or connected learning. Scholars in this area have proposed that women tend to learn differently; women learn through relationships with others, through nurturing and caring, and by connecting with each other (Belenky & Stanton, 2000). Belenky and Stanton critique traditional transformative learning theory on this and related bases. They suggest that although Mezirow presumed relations of equality among participants in discourse, most human relationships are asymmetrical. This has serious consequences, especially for women. Dualistic thinking (e.g., male/female, thinking/feeling, public/private) serves to create hierarchies in which one pole of the dichotomy is prized and the other devalued. We must, the authors have argued, replace dualistic categories with integrative thinking (as in connected and relational).

Drawing on Belenky's well-known earlier research with her colleagues (Belenky, Clinchy, Goldberger, & Tarule, 1986), Belenky and Stanton (2000) described six developmental stages of knowing for women: silenced, received knowers, subjective knowers, separate knowers, connected knowers, and constructivist knowers. It was the distinction between separate knowing and connected knowing that was of greatest interest to the authors in examining implications for transformative learning theory. The traditional theory, they suggested, places separate knowing in a central role. Unlike separate knowers, who follow lines of reasoning and look for flaws in logic to create more defensible knowledge, connected knowers suspend judgment and struggle to understand others' points of view. They look for strengths rather than weaknesses in another person's point of view. Belenky and Stanton wrote, "The more Connected Knowers disagree with another person the harder they will try to understand how that person could imagine such a thing, using empathy, imagination and storytelling as tools for entering into another's frame of mind" (p. 87). They saw this as a radically different stance in which the goal is to see holistically, not analytically.

Some recent research validates this understanding of transformative learning. Stuckey, Taylor, and Cranton (2014), in their project to develop a survey for assessing transformative learning outcomes and processes, recruited 136 adults to respond to a 110-item survey in their pilot project. Statistical analyses supported the existence of three scales related to connected or relational learning: emotions, support, and dialogue.

Kroth and Cranton (2014), using a narrative approach to understanding transformative learning, collected stories from 10 participants in a variety of contexts and cultures. They found that relationships played a major role in several of the stories, especially relationships with a spouse or other family members. E. W. Taylor and Snyder (2012), in their review of the literature on transformative learning, reported that relationships were becoming increasingly recognized as an important aspect of the transformative learning process.

Carter (2000) found that transformation occurred primarily through developmental relationships among the upper-level management women she studied. In describing several types of relationships reported on by her participants, Carter labeled one of these as a love relationship—a deep, intimate sharing of experiences and feelings over a sustained period of time. Others of Carter's participants maintained relationships in their memory with loved ones who had died. Gilly (2004) reported on an experience of transformative education among members of a doctoral peer group in which she found collaboration and relationship to be the central aspects of transformation.

English and Irving (2012) reviewed and analyzed the literature on women's transformative learning and noted that much of this writing was based on studies of women in oppressive conditions. They also emphasized that the studies they reviewed highlighted the importance of relationships in women's transformative experiences. I see some danger in proposing that women engage in transformative learning in a particular way. To suggest that women learn one way and men learn another way could be seen as stereotyping, and, given that women's learning is depicted as less valued in our society, this could also serve to further marginalize women. English (2004) spoke well to this issue in reporting on her study of women's learning in volunteer organizations. Perhaps the real problem here is that there is an insistence that each theoretical perspective is the "right one," or at least superior to the others.

Social Change

Transformative learning theory has long been criticized for not paying enough attention to social change. Although Mezirow (1990, 2000) drew on the works of Freire and Habermas, both of whom had social change as a central goal, Mezirow believed that individual transformation preceded social transformation. Collard and Law (1989), Cunningham (1992), and Hart (1990) were among those who objected to this view early on in the development of the theory.

Social reform has long been a goal of adult education. Two examples come immediately to mind. The first example is from Canada; the Antigonish Movement was founded by Father Jimmy Tompkins and Father Moses Coady in the late 1920s as a way of helping ordinary people foster economic development through cooperatives and credit unions. Using mass meetings, study groups, kitchen meetings, and community courses, the leaders of the movement sought to "help the people build greater and better democratic institutions" (Coady, 1939, p. 3), as reflected in the six principles of the Antigonish Movement (Coady, 1939):

1. Individual needs are primary and need to be developed in social contexts.
2. The root of social reform lies in education.
3. Individuals are most concerned with economic needs; education must start there.
4. Group settings are most suitable to education.
5. Social reform both causes and depends on change in social and economic institutions.
6. A full, self-actualized life for everyone in the community is the aim of the movement.

The second example, of course, is the Highland Folk School (now called the Highlander Research and Education Center) founded in the United States by Myles Horton and his colleagues in 1932. As was the case in the

Antigonish Movement, the goal was to provide education for ordinary people as a way of effecting social change. The development of literacy skills was considered one way of fostering both social and personal transformation. Horton's goal was to bring people together to challenge oppressive organizations and governments. Based on interviews with eight current educators from the Highlander Center, Ebert, Burford, and Brian (2003) described the following nine facets of practice relevant to transformative education:

1. Providing a safe place to encourage discourse and reflection
2. Assuming participants bring a wealth of knowledge and experience
3. Helping people discover they are not alone
4. Facilitating critical thinking
5. Helping people develop voice and the confidence to act
6. Solving problems through synergy
7. Encouraging lifelong and diverse learning for change
8. Promoting the idea that everyone is an important member of a community
9. Implementing continuous improvement (adapted from pp. 325–326)

Those writers and theorists who have emphasized social action see critical reflection without social action as "a self-indulgent form of speculation that makes no real difference to anything" (Brookfield, 2000, p. 143). More recently, Brookfield (2012) described transformative learning in relation to critical theory and explored "the learning that critical theory mandates and the degree to which this learning can be considered transformative" (p. 131). Mezirow (2000) distinguished between educational tasks—helping people become aware of oppressive structures and learn how to change them—and political tasks that force economic change. This distinction is helpful. Mezirow was not saying that social action is not the responsibility of adult educators or the product of transformative learning. He was saying that educators go about making a difference in the world by helping learners learn how to make a difference in the world. Still, this does not fully address the link between transformative learning and social action.

In a review of the work of bell hooks and Angela Davis, Brookfield (2003) concluded that both of these authors saw transformative learning as ideology critique. The purpose of transformative education was to "help people uncover and challenge dominant ideology and then learn how to organize social relations according to noncapitalist logic" (p. 224). In social action, disequilibrium is present in all relationships. Transformation includes not only structural change in the individual's way of seeing himself or herself and the world, but also structural change in the social world that provides the context for the individual's life.

In his writing on critical theory, Brookfield (2005, [2012]) took a similar stance. Ideology critique describes the ways in which people come to recognize uncritically assimilated assumptions and beliefs. The role of adult educators is to help people see how these ideologies (assumptions and beliefs) have been imposed on them without their knowledge and how they justify and maintain economic and political inequity (Brookfield, 2005, p. 13).

In their development (Cranton, p. 326) of a transformative learning survey, Stuckey and colleagues (2014) found four subscales that reflected the social change aspects of transformative learning: empowerment, social action, unveiling oppression, and ideology critique. These scales were consistent and reliable in the statistical analysis of the survey. Of the stories Kroth and Cranton (2014) collected, three were directly related to social change: the story of the experience of a veteran of the Iraq War; the story of an educator who worked on a project for North Korean students living in South Korea; and the story of helping Nigerian women understand the nature of their oppression at the hands of religious leaders, men in general, and the social norms of the culture.

Torres (2003) followed Freire's (1970) view of transformative learning as an instrument for social justice. He raised an interesting paradox. Democracy implies participation based on the assumption of equality among people. Yet people need to be educated in democratic participation. Knowing how to engage in discourse, collaborate with others, and exercise democratic rights and obligations is both a precondition and a product of democratic participation. Torres argued that "transformative social justice should be based on unveiling the conditions of alienation and exploitation in society, thereby creating the basis for the understanding and comprehension of the roots of social behaviour" (p. 429). He did not, however, deny the importance of what he called self-transformation, a process by which we rethink our past and gain an understanding of the formation of our self. Understanding our present condition allows us to see the limitations and possibilities of being a "self-in-the-world" (p. 429).

Groups and Organizations

Group and organizational transformation is another branch of inquiry in transformative learning theory. Yorks and Marsick (2000) have focused their research on action learning and collaborative inquiry, two group learning strategies employing reflection and action aimed at producing transformational organizational learning. Similarly, Kasl and Elias (2000) reported on transformative learning within the context of group learning and organizational change. It is sometimes difficult to distinguish between transformative learning with social change as a goal and group learning. Scott (2003) helped to clarify this when she said that "transformation includes structural changes in the psyches of persons and in the structures of society" (p. 281). Following Kegan's (2000) constructivist-developmental approach, Scott saw a collective movement occurring toward higher mental functions.

Although learning in groups has a long history in adult education, the idea that a group as an entity can learn is a different and novel one. Kasl, Marsick, and Dechant (1997) claimed that a group, as a system, can create knowledge for itself. The popular work on learning organizations follows this model. The idea began with the work of Argyris and Schon (1974) and was popularized by Senge (1990), among others. But it was the work of Watkins and Marsick (1993) that connected the learning organization to transformative learning. Yorks and Marsick's (2000) work on organizational transformation was based on action learning and collaborative inquiry. *Action learning* involves learning in small groups or teams by working on a real project or problem in the organization. *Collaborative inquiry* sounds similar—it is defined as a "process consisting of repeated episodes of reflection and action through which a group of peers strives to answer a question of importance to them" (p. 266). There is an emphasis on co-inquiry, democratic process, and holistic understanding of the experience. According to Yorks and Marsick, organizations transform along several dimensions: the nature of the environment, the vision or mission of the organization, the organization's products or services, the organizational structure, management of the organization, and how members of the organization see their roles.

Fenwick (1998) was quite critical of this perspective. She suggested that those who write about learning organizations are likely closely aligned with the organization's goals, but the visions and goals of the ordinary person working within the organization may be very different. She also argued that it is not reasonable to describe an organization as a unitary, intelligent entity. It is neither unitary nor bounded and stable—it contains multiple subgroups, different cultures, and a continually changing workforce.

Can groups learn and transform? Kasl and Elias's (2000) writing was based on the premise that they can. They used the following concepts to support this assumption: (a) individuals, groups, and organizations all share common characteristics and (b) the idea of a group mind. Kasl and Elias included both critical reflection and discernment as central processes in their conceptualization of transformative learning. Discernment begins with receptivity and appreciation and moves to seeing patterns of relational wholeness. "Frames of reference are transcended rather than analyzed" (Kasl & Elias, 2000, p. 231). Transformative learning becomes an expansion of consciousness that is collective as well as individual. Using a case study, Kasl and Elias illustrated that processes usually ascribed to individuals can provide a model for understanding and interpreting group learning.

Schapiro, Wasserman, and Gallegos (2012) brought together the literature on how groups provide a context for transformative learning. They described the group as a container for the dialogue that is essential to transformative learning and refer to three types of transformative learning groups: groups for personal growth and self-awareness, groups for relational empathy across differences, and groups for critical systemic consciousness.

Taking this notion into the organizational context, K. E. Watkins, Marsick, and Faller (2012) explored how transformative learning relates to organizational learning and development. They presented a model of facilitating transformative learning for organizational change that distinguished between a system perspective and an individual perspective in relation to the role of a leader. They acknowledged the complexity of fostering transformative learning in a complex global workplace and an uncertain economic climate, but the authors saw transformative learning theory as a significant way of creating responses that allow organizations to survive.

Ecological View

O'Sullivan and his colleagues from the Transformative Learning Centre at the Ontario Institute for Studies in Education provided an unusual and intriguing approach to transformative learning. Their broad vision spanned the individual, relational, group, institutional, societal, and global perspectives:

> Transformative learning involves experiencing a deep, structural shift in basic premises of thought, feelings, and actions. It is a shift of consciousness that dramatically and permanently alters our way of being in the world. This shift includes our understanding of ourselves and our self-locations and our relationships with other humans and with the natural world. It also involves our understanding of power relations in interlocking structures of class, race and gender, our body awareness, our visions of alternative approaches to living, and our sense of possibilities for social justice, peace, and personal joy. (Ontario Institute for Studies in Education, 2004)

O'Sullivan (2003) was careful to say that he did not see transformative learning as an individual process but rather a personal process that is carried out in "integrally webbed totalities" (p. 355). Central to his understanding was that we are part of the whole. We should strive for a planetary community that holds together without collapsing and obliterating human diversity.

A few years later, O'Sullivan (2012) said that "we live in a paradoxical moment," and "ours is a time of great possibilities and also of grave dangers"

(p. 162). He highlighted the dimensions of transformative learning that characterized the integrative nature of his work: holism, the wisdom of women, the wisdom of indigenous people, and spirituality. The description of these voices led him back to his earlier view that transformative education involves "experiencing a deep structural shift in the basic premises of our thoughts, feelings, and actions" (p. 175).

In Sweden, the Holma College of Integral Studies took a similar approach to understanding transformative learning (Gunnlaugson, 2003). The college provided a one-year intensive adult education program in personal and global well-being studies, drawing participants who were looking for personal and collective transformation. An emphasis on "learning to love life in all forms first, then extending this love out from the personal to more universal horizons" (p. 326) allowed students to develop what was described as an "integrally informed" education.

Extrarational Approach

The extrarational approach to transformative learning theory goes beyond Mezirow's cognitive understanding. Many of the writers in the field have been drawn to something beyond the cognitive way of processing, even without labeling it as extrarational (e.g., Herman, 2003; Lennard, Thompson, & Booth, 2003). If we can integrate this way of understanding transformation with Mezirow's work rather than treating it as an opposing position, I think we will have made good steps in the direction of developing an integrative holistic theory (Cranton & Roy, 2003).

Boyd and Myers (1988) were early proponents of using Jungian psychology to explain transformative learning (see also Boyd, 1985, 1989). They described a process of discernment in which symbols, images, and archetypes play a role in personal illumination. Boyd (1989) reported on a method of working in small groups in which individuals struggle to deal with unconscious content. The group itself affects the way individual members create images, identify personal dilemmas, and relate developmental phases to personal stages. Boyd defined *personal transformation* as "a fundamental change in one's personality involving conjointly the resolution of a personal dilemma and the expansion of consciousness resulting in greater personality integration" (p. 459). Boyd suggested that transformation is an inner journey of individuation, the process of learning through reflection on the psychic structures that make up one's uniqueness. That Boyd's early writing is frequently cited 20 years later shows how it resonates with many people's experience of transformation.

Dirkx (2001b) took up the torch of extending transformative learning theory beyond the ego-based, rational, and objective traditional approach.

Dirkx (1997) proposed that transformative learning involves very personal and imaginative ways of knowing—the way of mythos rather than logos. Dirkx drew on Hillman's (2000) and T. Moore's (1996) writings on soul and Jung's (1971) concept of individuation.

Transformative learning involves imaginative and emotional ways of knowing, said Dirkx (1997). Mythos reflects a facet of knowing that we can see in symbols, images, stories, and myths. Framing learning as a problem of critical self-reflection leads us to neglect the emotional, spiritual, and imaginative aspects of transformation and yields a limited, fragmented perspective rather than a holistic, whole-person understanding. Boyd (1991) talked of "transformative education" in order to maintain holism. Similarly, the founders of the *Journal of Transformative Education* chose that title deliberately to be inclusive, integrative, and holistic (Markos & McWhinney, 2004).

It is one thing to say this and another to understand what it means in relation to both theory and practice. Dirkx (1997) described *soul* through examples of experiences rather than through a definition—being awestruck by a sunset, gripped by pain and helplessness in the face of another's suffering. We experience soul through art, music, and film. It is that magic moment, a defining moment, which transcends rationality and gives depth, power, mystery, and deep meaning to the connection between the self and the world. In nurturing soul, we attend not only to the intellectual aspects of the learning environment but also to the emotional, spiritual, social, and physical aspects. We pay attention to the small, everyday occurrences (Dirkx, 2000); listen to individual and collective psyches; understand and appreciate images; and honor the multifaceted dimensions of learning.

Jung (1971, p. 448) defined *individuation* as the process by which individuals differentiate themselves from the general, collective society. It involves becoming aware of and considering the psychic structures of anima, animus, ego, shadow, and the collective unconscious. People come to see how they are both the same as and different from others. Transformation through individuation occurs whether we are conscious of it or not. However, when we participate in it consciously and imaginatively, we develop a deepened sense of self and an expansion of consciousness. Transformation is the emergence of the Self (in Jungian psychology *Self,* with a capital *S,* refers to the totality of psychic structures).

The process of individuation, becoming conscious of what is unique about oneself, involves differentiating ourselves from people we have admired and modeled ourselves on—parents, teachers, and mentors (Sharp, 2001). Individuality and group identity are incompatible. According to transformative learning theory, individuals come to question assumptions and perspectives that were uncritically absorbed from family, community, and culture. This sounds very much like differentiating ourselves from others upon whom we have modeled ourselves, except that according to Mezirow, it is a conscious, cognitive, rational, problem-solving process, and according to the Jungian perspective, it is an intuitive, emotional, and often not even a voluntary journey. Jung writes, "The developing personality obeys no caprice, no command, no insight, only brute necessity: it needs the motivating force of inner or outer fatalities" (cited in Sharp, 2001, p. 66).

As different as the paths are, it seems they are going to the same place. If we want, as we say we do, a holistic theory of transformative learning, then both paths can be valid. Those among us who strive to develop theories to explain others' learning are also human beings looking at ourselves and the world through the lens of our meaning perspectives. It should not be too surprising that this results in different ways of seeing the journey. Jung (1971), in his work on psychological type preferences (see Chapter 5), told the story of different people taking the same trip. One person may wax eloquently about the beauty of the landscape; another may focus on the restaurants in the area and describe the many good meals he had; someone else may have noticed neither the landscape nor the restaurants but had instead spent time getting to know the people and understanding their culture.

Toward an Integrated Theory

The fragmentation of transformative learning theory into several strands is helpful in our understanding of what can be considered to be transformative learning. But it is not helpful in theory development. To develop a comprehensive and consistent theory of transformative learning, we need to reflect on if and how these pieces fit together. In the introductory chapter to *The Handbook of Transformative Learning*, Cranton and Taylor (2012) explored this issue. They emphasized that we need to move away from dualisms (e.g., rational or extrarational, individual or social) and explore how the various perspectives can coexist and contribute to a meaningful theory. At the same time, we need to be conscious of Newman's (2012) valid critique of transformative learning theory as a theory that may not exist as an identifiable phenomenon but rather as just another way of talking about good teaching.

In Stuckey and colleagues' (2014) description of their transformative learning survey, they separated transformative learning outcomes from transformative learning processes. This may be helpful in understanding how an integrative theory can be developed. Based on a thorough literature review, they listed the outcomes of transformative learning, including acting differently, having a deeper self-awareness, holding more open perspectives, and experiencing a deep shift in worldview. The processes of transformative learning included cognitive/rational processes, extrarational processes, and processes related to social critique. Those processes that described relational learning were included in the extrarational processes. Group and organizational transformative learning could be cognitive, extrarational, or pertaining to social critique, depending on the circumstances. Stuckey and colleagues' (2014) thinking in the development of the survey was that regardless of the process, transformative learning led to the same outcomes. The goal was to develop an instrument that assessed both outcomes and processes.

A good theory takes into account a variety of circumstances and possibilities while remaining true to the meaning of the theory. Transformative learning certainly can take place through a cognitive or an intuitive process, as we see in the writings of Mezirow and Dirkx and others. Whether a person engages in a cognitive or extrarational process may depend on his or her personality characteristics (see Chapter 5) or on the circumstances of the learning. If I am engaged in transformative learning related to my work, it is perhaps more likely that this process is cognitive and rational. If I am struggling with the death of my son or the complexities of my relationship with a friend, the process may fall more into the extrarational area.

Similarly, whether the transformative learning process is an individual or a social justice endeavor depends on circumstances, and both are valid and reasonable ways of engaging in transformative learning. Individual transformative learning depends on a person calling into question her or his assumptions, beliefs, and values. Transformative learning related to social justice involves calling into question social norms, social values, and issues related to oppression, abuse, brutality, violence, and war. What is being questioned is different, but the process may be the same. And if we accept the definition of transformative learning, the outcome is a deep shift in perspective.

Research on Transformative Learning

With the International Conference on Transformative Learning in its 11th year and the *Journal of Transformative Education* in its 12th volume, the amount of accessible research on transformative learning has grown exponentially.

K. Taylor (2000) outlined eight themes from the research published before 2000:

1. Transformative learning is uniquely adult.
2. Transformative learning appears to be a linear, but not necessarily step-wise, process.
3. The nature of a frame of reference and how it transforms is unclear.

4. A disorienting dilemma usually initiates transformative learning.
5. Critical reflection is significant to transformative learning.
6. Discourse is equally dependent on relational ways of knowing.
7. Context plays an important role in shaping transformative learning, but the influence of culture has not been well investigated.
8. Some characteristics of a learning environment that fosters transformative learning have been identified, but more work needs to be done in this area. (As cited in Cranton, 2011, pp.331–332)

Essentially, the research supports Mezirow's (2000) theoretical description, with the possible exception of the importance of relational ways of knowing. However, even here, Mezirow (2003b) has now elaborated on the conditions of discourse to include interpersonal skills, social relationships, and emotional intelligence. We must keep in mind that Taylor chose to review only those studies that referred directly to Mezirow's conceptualization of transformative learning, though some studies also included other theoretical models.

Based on this review, Taylor suggested three future directions for research: (a) in-depth analyses of specific components of transformative learning that tend to be overlooked in the broader studies—for example, feelings such as anger, happiness, and shame; the management of emotions; and changes in behavior following transformation; (b) studies of how transformative learning is fostered in classrooms; and (c) new and varied research designs and data collection techniques, including longitudinal research, observer participation, collaborative inquiry, action research, and quantitative studies.

E. W. Taylor and Snyder (2012) have pointed out the constantly evolving nature of the research on transformative learning. In terms of methodology, they noted that the methodologies being used have changed over time to include action research, narrative inquiry, autoethnography, and case studies. Meta-analyses, mixed-methods approaches, and surveys have also taken an important place in the research literature. Interdisciplinary approaches have been growing, and collaborative inquiry is taking its place in the literature.

Summary

Transformative learning theory has benefited greatly over the years from the contributions of scholars from a variety of perspectives. Many researchers and writers have emphasized relational, connected knowing over individual, autonomous learning. From this perspective, transformative learning has a different emphasis and perhaps a different outcome. Subjective discussion (rather than rational discourse) encourages participants to share their experiences in a nonjudgmental way, and connected knowing involves working hard to understand others rather than looking for flaws in others' reasoning.

Social change lies at the heart of the history of adult education. In the 1920s and 1930s, adult education practice and theory was about helping people challenge oppressive organizations and governments. Those who have criticized Mezirow's work on the basis of his ignoring social action as a goal of transformative learning may have overlooked his desire to help people learn how to change oppressive structures rather than to change them himself—his distinction between educational and political tasks—as well as his own commitment to that work. Nevertheless, it is the case that adult education theory in general, and transformative learning theory in particular, has moved away from social issues and toward an emphasis on individual learning in recent decades. Brookfield's (2005) four traditions of criticality are helpful in understanding how both personal and social transformation are a part of what we do in adult education.

The idea that groups and organizations as entities can learn and transform provides yet another perspective on the theory (Kasl & Elias, 2000; Schapiro et al., 2012). I accept that groups and organizations change and develop, but I question the concept of a "group mind," and therefore I question the idea that groups transform in the way individuals transform. Group transformation is an intriguing idea, but I think it needs to be better situated in transformative learning theory or perhaps named differently.

O'Sullivan's broad vision of transformative learning theory, with its goal of striving for a planetary community, may have the potential of opening up our understanding of transformation so as to integrate all perspectives. I suggest that we need to explore how this vision is related to the existing alternative ways of describing transformation.

The extrarational approach put forth by Dirkx and others provides us with an intriguing and complementary way of understanding the central process of transformation. It brings in imagination, intuition, soul work, and emotion as ways in which people come to see themselves and their world in a new light. As different as the extrarational approach is from Mezirow's cognitive, rational description of transformative learning, the two need not be viewed as contradictory (Dirkx, Mezirow, & Cranton, 2006).

I do not intend to gloss over the differences between these viewpoints—the processes involved and the expected outcomes of each are fundamentally different. For example, if one views transformation as individuation, the outcome is self-knowledge and a more individuated personality. But each of these ways of understanding transformation can be descriptive of the experiences of different individuals or even of the same individual on different occasions.

Transformative learning theory is a theory in progress in terms of not only how people are thinking about and elaborating on it but also how the expanding body of research is supporting and asking questions of the theoretical developments. Much of the research supports Mezirow's understanding of transformation, but that may be in part because the reviews we rely on to make sense out of the field emphasize studies that are based on this approach. Research that includes spirituality, relational knowing, and authenticity are beginning to help us grasp how the various perspectives complement and elaborate on each other. Perhaps most importantly, those individuals who are involved in the continued development of transformative learning theory are engaged in intentional efforts to expand our thinking.

4

TRANSFORMATION

The Learner's Story

In this chapter, I examine the process of transformative learning from the learner's point of view. In our project, Michael Kroth and I collected 10 first-person stories of transformative learning (Kroth & Cranton, 2014). We invited current students, former students, and colleagues to tell us about their transformative learning experiences. Two of the stories were based on psychological dilemmas, two were responses to loss and trauma, two were the products of educational experiences, two occurred in the context of social change, and two described experiences related to spirituality. This range reflects the different perspectives on transformative learning, and it also reflects the various kinds of habits of mind that are revised.

It is not just individual differences that come into play here. Transformative learning takes place in a multiplicity of contexts, it is stimulated by different types of events, and it occurs in relation to a variety of kinds of habits of minds. Studies have been conducted in higher education settings, informal learning contexts, and organizations (E. W. Taylor & Snyder, 2012). The transformative process can be provoked by a single dramatic event, a series of almost unnoticed cumulative events, a deliberate conscious effort to make a change in one's life, or the natural developmental progression of becoming more mature. Transformative learning can deal with a person's personal or professional life and can be quite different between the two contexts. Whether the habits of mind under revision are psychological, sociolinguistic, epistemic, moral-ethical, philosophical, or aesthetic may well determine how the learning is felt and experienced.

Because it is not just one story, and because I believe there are helpful patterns to be understood, I explore the learner's transformative learning process from two dimensions in this chapter. First, I consider the process from the dimension of ways of knowing—the critical reflection perspectives and the extrarational perspectives. Second, I consider the temporal frames in which these ways of knowing may occur—epochal, incremental, and developmental.

Ways of Knowing: The Critical Self-Reflection Perspective

Mezirow (1991, 2000, 2012) described transformative learning in terms of phases in which critical reflection and critical self-reflection and discourse play central roles (see Chapter 2). Most writers have been careful to say that the models of the transformative learning process based on phases have not been intended to imply that the phases are linear, discrete, or independent. That is, a person may cycle through some phases more than once, may skip some steps, or may experience aspects of the process in varying orders. However, the very nature of the models does imply some order and some linearity. You are more likely to reintegrate at the end, and you are more likely to be disoriented at the beginning, though both disorientation and reintegration may occur at other times in the process.

There is a good body of research to support this perspective, especially among researchers who have used Mezirow's writing as their theoretical framework. For example, E. W. Taylor and Snyder (2012) reported that Mezirow's phases of transformative learning have been generally confirmed by some studies, but at the same time they have called for researchers to look beyond Mezirow's conceptualization of the theory. I now follow this through from the point of view of the learner experiencing transformation. I generally stay with Mezirow's phases, but I shorten and adapt them somewhat based on my own thinking about the process and my observations of and conversations with students.

Empowerment

Learner empowerment is both a goal of and a condition for transformative learning. An empowered learner is able to fully and freely engage in critical reflection, participate in discourse, and act on revised perspectives. A person who is oppressed, in need of shelter or food, depressed, or feeling trapped in his or her circumstances may not be able to respond to events in a potentially transformative way (Mezirow, 2012). Yet unbearable social conditions can also provoke transformative learning (Kucukaydin, 2010; Wiessner, 2000), and Frankl (1984) has shown us we can achieve transformation under any conditions. It is this paradox that has led some writers to argue that changes in social conditions must precede individual transformation.

David was a student in an introductory undergraduate adult education course I was facilitating. At the time I knew him, he was in his mid- or late

50s; was a slight, gentle man and had a hesitant way of speaking and an obviously shy nature. He mostly sat in class with his baseball cap pulled down low over his eyes, watching others carefully out from under the bill of the cap. I later learned that David was registered as a special student—he had not yet been admitted to the program—but at the time, I didn't realize this. David believed that he would be able to transfer credit from the courses he took as a special student to the degree program once he was admitted. He had been told that he needed to maintain grades of B or higher to be accepted into the program.

David had a varied background. While he was in the course with me, he was driving a truck on a night shift to pay for his tuition and his living expenses. He dreamed of becoming an educator. David's writing was always refreshing and innovative in style and content, but he participated little in class.

I am not sure how many courses he took before he was told he could not come into the program, but I think it was at least five or six. He took two with me, but he fared less well in other courses, and he never had the courage to ask how he could improve his marks or to question his probationary position in the program. It was a financial struggle for him to pay his tuition and buy his books; in the end, all was lost.

David quietly left, refusing my and others' offers to help or to see what could be done. He felt completely powerless in the face of this academic world and its unfathomable policies and procedures. I do not know where David is now, but I think of him often. If someone, including me, had been able to discover what was going on a bit earlier, I suspect his story would have turned out differently. David did not feel empowered, and he could not act on his own behalf.

Disorienting Event

The literature contains some descriptions of the types of activities and approaches that educators might use in order to stimulate critical reflection (Brookfield, 1995; Gozawa, 2003; Kreber, 2012). I discuss these in Chapter 7. Even when an educator deliberately sets up circumstances to promote critical reflection, not everyone or perhaps not anyone will be affected by it. Outside of the classroom context, critical reflection can be stimulated by any encounter with an unexpected or contradictory point of view. It can come through a book, a discussion with a friend, an unusual or tragic event, a change in work context, or a sudden insight.

I met Sheila when I was working in a management development program for a federal government department. My role was to help people interpret the results of a performance appraisal that included staff, supervisor, and self-ratings and then to help the individual set up a plan for professional development. Sheila had prided herself on being task oriented, running a tight ship, and getting the work done. She thought she had collegial (if distant) relationships with her staff. She did not socialize with her staff, nor did she want to. Sheila's self-evaluation was good, as was her supervisor's evaluation of her management skills. However, her staff ratings were in the lowest range possible, and staff open-ended comments indicated that they found Sheila to be arrogant, uncaring, unsupportive, and uninterested in their work or them as people. Sheila was so devastated by these unexpected results that she thought seriously about leaving her position. She had encountered perceptions of her performance at work that were completely at odds with how she saw herself.

I worked with Sheila to help her set a series of goals, strategies for meeting them, and ways to get ongoing feedback from her staff. When I heard a year or so later that she had transferred to another government office, I assumed that the appraisal process had left her feeling there was nothing she could do. I found out, though, that Sheila had indeed transformed her perspective on the manager's role and had made profound changes in her practice even though this had to be, for her, in a new location. Her personal confidence carried her through once the initial shock of the unexpected feedback abated; she felt empowered, and she was able to examine and question her practice in a careful and productive way. I do not know for sure, but I suspect that Sheila's learning was more incremental than epochal, even though the event that precipitated it was completely unexpected.

Events that stimulate critical reflection can take many forms. Being confronted with knowledge that directly contradicts previous accepted knowledge leads us to question what we thought we knew. We tend to accept, without question, knowledge acquired from sources like teachers, doctors, writers, and religious authorities, and that knowledge becomes embedded as an uncritically assimilated habit of mind. Encountering perspectives that challenge previously accepted knowledge can come from many different sources—a novel, a film, a poem, artwork, or a discussion with others.

Exposure to social norms other than those to which we subscribe can be a disorienting event. Social norms and expectations are often so deeply entrenched that we are not even aware of their presence. When I ask my students to evaluate their learning and select a grade that represents that evaluation, this often contradicts their prior educational experiences and their notion of the roles of teacher and learner. They may say they cannot do it, they had never imagined such a thing, and surely such a practice destroys academic standards and the quality of the entire educational system. They simply had never thought of the possibility of their being able to judge their own learning.

Larger societal and political events may provoke critical reflection for some individuals. The events of September 11, 2001; the U.S. wars in Iraq and Afghanistan; and the kidnapping of hundreds of girls in Nigeria are just a few examples of situations that have led people to engage in critical reflection on their beliefs, values, and perceptions of government leaders.

Life crises—a loved one dying, a marriage breaking up, losing a job, experiencing financial ruin—or positive changes—receiving a promotion, entering retirement, completing a years-long project—can challenge individuals to reconsider their values, expectations, moral positions, or self-concepts. Sometimes, when I see graduate students delaying completion of a thesis, I suspect they are unconsciously avoiding the change in lifestyle that will take place once that life-consuming task is done. Traumatic crises may not lead to critical self-reflection if the person feels disempowered by the event, or it just may take some time for reflection to be possible.

Alyssa's story (in Kroth & Cranton, 2014) started with the death of her father, but this was only the beginning of a multilayered experience. Alyssa responded to her mother's reaction to her father's death, writing that "this story is about the transformation I witnessed in my mother after my father's death. More than a personal change in her, it was an enlightening change in the way I saw my mother" (p. 48). It was not until her father died that Alyssa saw her mother as her own person.

Questioning Assumptions and Perspectives

At the heart of Mezirow's (2000, 2012) theory of transformative learning is critical reflection and critical self-reflection—questioning assumptions and perspectives. People become aware of assumptions, make them explicit, consider the sources of the assumptions and the consequences of holding them, and question their validity. As I described in Chapter 2, this can also be framed by content, process, and premise reflection.

Becoming aware of assumptions or the habits of mind that consist of a web of related assumptions is difficult. These things are a part of the fabric of who we are or who we perceive we are. We act on them without thought. Even when we suspect that something might be wrong with how we see ourselves or the world around us, it is hard to admit, let alone bring it out into the open and turn it around and look at it from different angles.

A good educator, community developer, counselor, therapist, or other helping professional can listen and then ask the kinds of questions that help an individual critically reflect on his or her habits of mind. I discuss this more fully in Chapter 7.

Sam is a professional athlete who is taking an online education course with me. His goal is to become a coach, and he hopes to learn about teaching techniques that can help him to get a job as a coach. The online course is based on discussion, interaction among group members, weekly activities, and the co-construction of knowledge among participants. This is not at all what Sam expected. He expected me, the teacher, to provide him with knowledge, which is not an unusual expectation of what a teacher does. Sam became quite aggressive about his expectations and my unwillingness to meet them.

I accepted his point of view as a reasonable one, given that this is a social norm in our culture, but I did not change what I was doing. I cannot presume to know what was going on in Sam's mind during this time, but I think he may have been influenced by the other participants in the course not responding to his postings. Perhaps it was also the case that my unwillingness to engage led him to stop and reflect.

After two or three weeks, Sam started responding to the weekly activities, and he commented on some other participants' postings. I responded to him. Other participants also responded to him. This course is still under way at the time of my writing, but I am fairly certain that Sam is questioning some of his assumptions about the role of teachers.

In another example, Sheared, in a symposium at the Adult Education Research Conference (Brookfield, Sheared, Johnson-Bailey, & Colin, 2005), described growing up as a female African American child in the southern United States where she did not realize she was marginalized. Later in life, she came to understand how race influences how others view a person. This understanding generalized to Sheared's interpretation of the literature and the media.

Discourse, Dialogue, and Support

As I discuss in Chapter 2 and as I mention repeatedly throughout this section, discourse, dialogue, and support from others appear to play a major role in transformative learning. Mezirow (2003b) defined *discourse* as "dialogue involving the assessment of beliefs, feelings, and values" (p. 59). He saw creating the conditions for transformative learning, including critical reflection and discourse, as being the essence of adult education and the defining characteristic of the role of the adult educator. Through discourse, we can see our points of view from the perspectives of others, which opens us up to critical questioning.

There are varied roles that others (educators, peers, friends, colleagues) play in transformative learning. Most obviously, perhaps, people play a role in questioning and challenging, helping us to unearth our hidden assumptions and question their validity. A friend may ask a friend, "Is it really necessary for you to talk to your adult son daily on the telephone?" and thereby encourage her to notice a potentially overly dependent relationship. An educator may ask students to write letters or participate in a debate from a point of view opposite to their own, promoting awareness of their reasons for holding that view. Others can assist us in not only articulating our own perspectives but also seeing alternatives.

Dialogue and support play vital roles in helping individuals maintain a good sense of self during a time when they may be making unsettling changes in the way they see themselves. In the research conducted by Stuckey, Taylor, and Cranton (2014), dialogue and support formed two scales in the extrarational perspective on transformative learning theory. This may involve general support of the "you are okay" variety, but it may also be specific feedback on changes that a learner is considering or in the process of making. Educators especially need to be aware of learners' needs for supportive and challenging feedback during transformative learning. Mezirow (1991) said that it is unethical to engage in transformative learning if we are not willing to support learners as they go through it.

There are so many learners' stories that could be told here. I think of Angela, who, on the last day of a five-day workshop on transformative learning, offered to make a presentation about her father's death, which had occurred several years earlier. Using photos and collages, she cried as she told her story for the very first time to this supportive group—she had been unable to speak of it before. I think of Lois, an independent and articulate woman who managed a large household, full-time studies, and part-time work and was terrified to the point of paralysis at the notion of making a presentation to her peers. With the help of dialogue, rehearsal, and feedback, she managed to overcome that fear and speak about a work of art she had created. And I think of Yeshey, who was chosen by her home government in Bhutan to come to Canada to learn about alternative perspectives on education. Yeshey relied on the support of her fellow Bhutanese students in this strange country, and she gradually formed alliances with Canadian educators.

Ways of Knowing: The Extrarational Perspective

Whether it is expressed as despair or joy, conflict or harmony, or anger or delight, dramatic opportunities for transformative learning exist when we are able to engage imaginatively with life's events (Dirkx, 2001a). Dirkx relayed several anecdotes to illustrate what he meant—a frustrated GED student who would rather be doing pottery than studying math, an individual whose readings on adult development theory illuminated her own life, a community college instructor who was resigned to not having time for collaborative work. Dirkx (2012) referred to soul work as the "imaginal method" (p. 124), including the use of emotion-laden images and the careful observation of these images (the context, feelings, relationships, and interactions). Components of the imaginal method include the process of association (recognization how the image reflects similar experiences from the past), amplification (making connections to popular culture, literature, and mythology), and animation (engaging in dialogue with the image). In his earlier writing, Dirkx advocated the use of journal writing, artistic projects, novels, and poetry—essentially any strategy that connects learners to soul work, which he described as critical to personal transformation (Dirkx, 2001b).

Our classrooms and workshop venues are not typically places where we encourage or even allow emotions, imagination, and fantasy. It is a common habit of mind to view educational contexts as places for the presentation of information and serious, rational discussion. We avoid or smooth over conflict; we bring things "back on track" when someone becomes fanciful. When I first encountered Dirkx's work, I needed to examine my discomfort. As a young student, I never had the courage to even speak in a class, never mind to express emotion or display imagination, and throughout my teaching career, being quiet, reflective, and analytical has been natural for me. Yet I am drawn to matters of the soul and am now convinced of the importance of working with images and feelings in fostering transformative learning. I have long encouraged journal writing, and in recent years I have also encouraged artistic projects of all kinds and incorporated movies, music, and fiction into my classes. There is no doubt that these activities are transformative for many students. What I still struggle with is letting the moment "be" when there is anger, fear, conflict, or despair—"facilitating transformative learning in which emotional reactions to the text are regarded as imagistic manifestations of inner selves" (Dirkx, 2001a, p. 15). The process of transformative learning can feel quite threatening when it brings into question the identity, or an identity, through which we have interacted with ourselves and the world.

How does this look and feel from the learner's perspective? Feller and colleagues (2004) described the experiences of Cohort 14 in which transformative learning was regarded as a practice of wholeness—a balance of mind, body, spirit, and emotion. Among a wide range of diverse experiences, participants kept journals, learned through the body by going for walks or meditating, engaged in spiritual activities such as lighting a candle and visualizing members of the group, and practiced specialized forms of dialogue designed to foster sharing and trust. Unfortunately, aside from telling us what they did and integrating this into a quadrinity model, the authors did not describe how they experienced transformative learning.

Sawyer (2003) told the story of Dr. Bruce Lipton, a cellular biologist who experienced a deep paradigm shift from a reductionist, determinist world-view to a quantum physics–based understanding, one founded on holism and uncertainty. For Lipton, this was an uninvited conversion from being nonspiritual to becoming a fully spiritual person. He felt "overwhelmed with joy and exhilaration" (p. 372) and felt compelled to share his discovery with others at 2:15 a.m.

Kasl and Yorks (2012) used the concept of presentational knowing to describe how transformative learning is fostered through intuitive and imaginal processes. Kasl gave us an illustrative story of presentational knowing and analyzed her experience vividly. She described how a lump of clay turned into a shape that was a figure of a woman, and how she saw this figure as a "woman emerging" (p. 506). She wrote, "Looking back, I now know that . . . I was beginning a three-year experience of transformative learning" (p. 507).

I remember Jim from three or four summers ago. I have told this story on different occasions; the most memorable telling was at a workshop on storytelling facilitated by Jo Tyler at Teachers College. Jim was probably the oldest person in the group of students taking an adult education methods course, and he obviously had a long-held fear of being "in school." For the first week and a half, Jim was the class clown. He was friendly and funny; he found a joke in everything we did. We all liked Jim very much, but I was also uncomfortable with how Jim used his clown role to avoid anything that might get serious. I no longer remember the exact circumstances that led to Jim's dramatic moment, but it was one of those everyday occurrences to which Dirkx (2000) suggested we pay attention. Jim suddenly shouted out, "I can't do this, I can't be a teacher, this was not meant to be, I am quitting now." We were stunned. I thought, "What did I say? What did I do?" and I could see the same questions in others' faces. It was a beautiful summer day. The sun was shining into our classroom windows, and someone was going by with a lawn mower. The only thing I could think to do was to break and somehow acknowledge Jim's moment. I suggested that we walk in the nearby woods and just ponder what we were all doing here. I knew Jim was not con-nected to me; he was much more comfortable in the presence of men. As we were leaving the classroom, I quietly asked two or three of the men in the group to walk with Jim.

We wandered for half an hour or so. I did not speak to Jim. I sensed I should not. But I participated by walking and pondering with others. After class, a group of the men took Jim to play miniature golf, then to a local pub for a meal, and then back to the residence for an evening of talk. The next day, Jim came to me and said he thought that "it would be okay," that he could do it after all. He dropped the clown role. He participated in serious dialogue, he became open about his fears, and he confessed to me that he was terrified of writing anything. I think this was an extrarational transformative experience.

Many of my students have experienced transformative learning through artistic learning projects. I have seen innumerable wonderful creations and listened to the stories accompanying them. It is hard to choose which story to tell, but Lisa's experience stands out for me. In a weeklong workshop on transformative learning, Lisa decided to create a collage to represent her transformative experiences. Lisa was a music teacher, but she had never worked with the visual arts. She described how she set up a space in her New York apartment for her collage and how she looked forward to working on the project each day. "The time flew," she said. "The hours disappeared when I worked on the collage." After the week's end, Lisa sent me digital photos of her collage, and we discussed her use of color, the images and symbols she included, and the meaning of the work for her. It was about two months later when I received a long and enthusiastic e-mail from Lisa. She had a new CD coming out, and when asked about the cover of the CD, she immediately thought of her collage. The collage would become the CD cover. But more than that, Lisa wrote about the depth of her experience in creating the collage, how she saw herself in a different way, and her changed perspective on the meaning of art and music and the connection between the two.

When I think about the numerous sculptures, paintings, poems, short stories, music CDs, quilts, stained glass works, kaleidoscopes, and collages that I have been honored to see in my practice, I am struck by the transformative learning process inherent in these projects. It certainly does not involve a reasoned, critically reflective progression. The transformative experience may be a flash of insight, a profoundly moving moment in which a person's view of himself or herself and the world is changed, or it may be a slow unfolding of the creative process revealed nonverbally, moving from tacit to explicit. In all of her writing, Greene (1995) eloquently invited educators to restructure and enhance learning experiences through the imagination and the arts.

The Temporal Dimension: Incremental or Epochal

Mezirow (2012) distinguished between transformative learning that occurs gradually over time (incremental) and that which is a sudden and dramatic change in perspective (epochal). Incremental transformation creeps up on a person over months or even years, perhaps partly or mostly an unconscious process, until the day when he or she looks back and says, "I was a different person then." From the transformative stories I hear in my practice and from my own experience, it seems that transformative learning is more often incremental than epochal. Research that describes transformative processes usually focuses on some defined period of time, such as a three-week residential program (Cohen, 2004) or a three-year slice of people's professional lives (Cranton & Carusetta, 2004b). Such research examines transformation during that time period, so it does not ask about gradual and dramatic changes in perspective. In K. Taylor's (2000) review of the research on transformative learning, he suggested that even "trigger events" or "initial reactions" extend over a period of time rather than being dramatic moments.

Because it is Mezirow who proposed that there are both epochal and incremental transformative experiences and because it is also Mezirow who approached transformative learning theory from a critically reflective, problem-solving perspective, we can only assume that even the epochal experience is not one of sudden illumination, the lightbulb appearing over the person's head. Even if the precipitating event is abrupt, it seems to be followed by a process of unfolding, including critical reflection, discourse, and a conscious revision of assumptions.

It seems that there are several possibilities here:

- A traumatic event that initiates a careful, reasoned exploration of values and beliefs and leads to a changed perspective
- A traumatic event that lies dormant for a long period of time and only gradually leads a person to change
- A deeply felt, positive experience or series of positive experiences that leads to a questioning of either personal habits of mind or perspectives on the world
- A sudden, disturbing experience that leads to an immediate and nonrational switch in beliefs
- A gradual, unnoticed, and perhaps not entirely conscious process of change over time that is recognized only in retrospect
- A series of small life changes, none of which are dramatic in themselves, but that lead cumulatively to a revision in a habit of mind over time
- A deliberate, conscious effort over time to change oneself and the way one sees the world

Whether we choose to define all of these as *transformative learning* would depend on our theoretical perspective.

In Anna Quindlen's (2002) novel *Blessings*, Skip has just been released from jail, where he was serving time for robbery. Skip has deeply embedded assumptions about himself and others—you just do not get out of the life you were born into. He sees this in the stories of his peers and people in the small community where he lives. People do not move from being trash to being upstanding citizens, from poverty to wealth, from unemployment to respectable work. When a days-old infant is left on Skip's doorstep, he knows this was meant to be. This baby is his to care for. He learns the practical things he needs to know, buys a book on baby care, and goes to a Walmart in a nearby town (where he will not be recognized) to buy the things a baby needs. Initially, it is a matter of sheer survival. Skip does not think about why he is doing what he is doing. He suffers through the sleepless nights; manages to hide the baby as he is working as a caretaker; avoids his former pub mates; and, in spite of his exhaustion and fear, delights in her first smile and the way she holds his finger. Skip finds support in unlikely places—his tough, dictatorial, over-80 employer and the daughter of his employer's maid. He dreams of a future where the baby grows up and goes to school, where he has a house and perhaps a small business. And then he begins to see that a person can get out of the life he was seemingly born into. If there is a reason for doing it—and the baby is his reason—a person can change. Skip's worldview is transformed. Even though misunderstanding and tragedy visit him again, Skip sees himself and the world around him in a new way.

In the summer program in which I facilitate the journey of trades and technical people into the world of teaching, there usually are no such disturbing events in people's lives, even though the move from practicing a trade to teaching that trade could certainly be described as a major life transition. But there are no babies left on doorsteps. Everyone has deliberately chosen to enter the teaching profession after thought, reflection, and discussion. My course is one of several courses for a mandatory (if they wish to teach in the community college system) certificate in adult education, and it is the second and last summer course. For many of the participants, the program and perhaps this last summer course is a transformative experience; I hear their stories and read their journals every year, and people often keep in touch with me and their classmates long after the program's end. Research shows, too, that many of the students engaging in this transition see it as transformative (Cranton, 2009).

We are together six hours a day for three weeks. Participants choose the topics they wish to explore; I provide the readings and design most of the learning activities (except usually in the last week, when the students lead several of the learning activities). Often, there is no sudden and dramatic change, but there is, day by day, one after another, a series of different points of view, questions, challenges to perceptions of what teaching means, sharing of experiences, and dialogue about educational practice. It is when people are nearing the end of the program and sometimes after they have returned to their colleges that they see and are able to describe their experience as transformative. To me, this is incremental transformation.

The Temporal Dimension: Developmental Transformation

From the developmental perspective, transformative learning takes place through the negotiation of developmental transitions (K. Taylor & Elias, 2012). K. Taylor and Elias followed Kegan's (1994) model of transformations of consciousness that "describes lifespan development in terms of increasing epistemological complexity" (p. 147). K. Taylor and Elias described this as a way of helping adult educators to encourage learners "perceive, feel, understand, act, relate, and *know* in ways more responsive to the crises our species must address" (p. 147, italics in the original). In his classic work, Tennant (1993) proposed that transformative learning occurs along with or as a part of normal life transitions. Most adult development models describe stages of development in which people move from black-and-white, authority-based thinking through to complex, integrative, weblike thinking in which there is no objective truth outside of the self, as Kegan did. Kegan (2000) proposed five increasingly complex epistemologies that begin with perceptions and move through to abstractions (the socialized mind) and abstract systems (the self-authoring mind) to the dialectical (the self-transforming mind). In the most complex epistemology, people create a distance from their own internal theories and perspectives so that they can recognize their incompleteness and embrace contradictory systems simultaneously. Kegan's approach did not depend on initiating or triggering events, although he did suggest that the modern social world demands increasingly complex ways of making meaning out of experience.

Based on the literature and extensive consultation with adult educators, K. Taylor (2000) described dimensions of development from the learner's perspective. She organized 36 characteristics into five dimensions summarized as follows:

1. Toward knowing as a dialogical process (inquiring into and responding to others' ideas, pursuing the possibility of objective truth)
2. Toward a dialogical relationship to oneself (exploring experience through a framework of analysis, making meaning of life stories within contexts)
3. Toward being a continuous learner (challenging oneself to learn in new realms, drawing on multiple capacities for learning)
4. Toward self-agency and self-authorship (accepting responsibility for choices, distinguishing what one has created for oneself from what is imposed by social forces)
5. Toward connection with others (experiencing oneself as a part of something larger, contributing to a collective endeavor)

Tennant (2012), who has long written about developmental perspectives on transformative learning, explored how different conceptualizations of selfhood help us realize our understanding of personal change. He wrote about the authentic self, the autonomous self, the repressed self, the socially constructed self, and the storied self, analyzing the implications for learning. The *authentic self* implies that there is an essence of the self that can be distorted by social forces. As in transformative learning theory, it is assumed that there is a true self that can be discovered when individuals question the distorting influence of their social roles. The *autonomous self* is "characterized by agency, choice, reflection, and rationality" (p. 35). The emphasis is on independence and self-control, as is the case in self-directed learning, and is related to personal empowerment. The *repressed self* is represented by the unconscious, meaning that we have motives, thoughts, and feelings of which we are unaware. Dirkx's (2012) interpretation of transformation through the lens of Jungian psychology illustrates this dimension. The *socially constructed self* takes into account the social context in understanding the individual. The course of individual development is shaped by social conventions. The *storied self* reflects the current strong interest in narratives and stories as a way of understanding transformative learning (C. Clark & Rossiter, 2009; Kroth & Cranton, 2014). We use stories to understand our lives and foster our questioning of our values and assumptions.

Summary

It has been an interesting experience for me, in writing this chapter, to read descriptions of how learners perceive transformative learning in the literature, to remember and attempt to articulate the experiences of students in my classes, and to push myself into considering transformative experience from the inside using alternative perspectives to the familiar and comfortable cognitive perspective.

We know quite a lot about what transformation looks like from the learner's perspective when we view the process as one with critical self-reflection and discourse at its center. More research has examined this way of understanding transformative learning than other ways of understanding. In this chapter, I have discussed what experiencing disorienting events, questioning assumptions and perspectives, and practicing discourse, dialogue, and support look like from the point of view of the person engaged in those processes.

With the help of Dirkx's writing (2012) and the experiences of students I have worked with, I have explored extrarational transformative learning from the learner's perspective. The joy, fear, exhilaration, and wholeness of the intersection of mind, body, and spirit come through in people's descriptions, though in many ways, it is beyond language and difficult to capture in a linear string of words. I hope I have managed to portray something of how people feel when they work outside the realm of cognitive rationality and find deep, powerful shifts in the way they see themselves and the world.

Both rational and extrarational transformation can occur suddenly and dramatically, gradually over time, or as a developmental process. The research tends to reveal primarily gradual, incremental experiences, though the appeal of the burning bush phenomenon is strong. When we tell stories about transformative experiences, it is more appealing to emphasize the dramatic. In the end, however, it seems that from the perspective of the person experiencing transformation, it is more often a gradual accumulation of ordinary experiences that leads to a deep shift in thinking, a shift that may become clear only when it is over.

The developmental theorists have all described, in one form or another, the movement from simple to increasingly complex ways of seeing the world. To use Mezirow's language, as people transform habits of mind, they acquire perspectives that are more open, permeable, and better justified. I especially enjoyed Tennant's discussion of the learning self from a variety of developmental perspectives.

In order to better understand the developmental perspective on transformative learning, we may need longitudinal studies of transformative learning and studies in which the researcher is present during the experience (e.g., studies of teaching experiences). It seems that narrative inquiry and storytelling would be a useful avenue to explore in order to understand learners' perspectives.

5

INDIVIDUAL DIFFERENCES

In his classic book on personality types, Daryl Sharp (1987), a Canadian Jungian analyst, included an amusing appendix in which he described a dinner party. The people attending the dinner party each demonstrate a different personality type based on Jung's model of psychological type. The charming hostess expresses her joy at gathering together her dear friends in a warm and welcoming manner. The host is an art historian who collects books, but he does not delve deeply into their content. The first guest is a defense lawyer; her arguments are based on logic and concrete facts in a well-organized manner. Another guest is a leading industrialist who is responsible for a large number of employees and finds the time to oversee every detail of the operation. The industrialist's wife is quiet and reserved, seeming to have a mysterious depth; she does not express her emotions often. A professor of medicine is another guest, well known for his boring lectures. He does not relate well to his students or to his patients. An engineer at the dinner party is full of new ideas and completely immersed in the possibilities of his ideas. He seems unaware of the reality of the world he lives in. And finally, there is a young poet who forgot to come to the dinner party as he was absorbed in his manuscript.

Sharp's delightful descriptions tend to simplify the differences among the eople at the dinner party, but when viewed as caricatures, they capture the essence of the variety of ways of being encountered in any context.

Transformative learning theory is based on a constructivist view of the world. In the constructivist view, people participate in the construction of reality, and this construction occurs within a context that influences it. Commonly accepted views are socially constructed, and understanding depends on a social process; people can attend to complex communications and organize complexity, and human interactions are based on social roles with implicit rules. In other words, we see the world through a lens constructed in our interaction with our social context. We also make decisions related to our perceptions in our own way. We are individuals living in and influenced by our social world, and we are individuals with important differences among us in the way we live, learn, work, and develop.

The literature in education contains many ways of classifying and explaining individual differences. Developmental phase, learning style, multiple intelligences, personality type, cognitive style, past experience, and self-directed learning readiness are just some of the ways in which writers try to account for learners' behavior and to predict how they will behave in the future. Many of these attempts to classify learners lead to dichotomies or mutually exclusive categories. People are described as visual learners or auditory learners; they are in the leaving-home phase or the moving-into-the-adult-world phase. There is value in this; we need patterns and commonalities and trends in order to make sense of things. However, we could also overlook the diversity and complexity of human learning if we are too rigid in our classification schemes.

Psychological type theory (Jung, 1971) is a meaningful way of understanding individual differences without oversimplification. Jung was clear that his study of psychological type was constructivist in nature. He wrote that "constructive means building up" (p. 422) and that he used constructivism as an approach that was the "antithesis of the reductive" (p. 422). Unfortunately, many of the inventories based on Jung's work do stereotype, but Jung accepted that individuals construct their own meaning of the world. At the same time, he attempted to classify these differences without losing their complexity.

In this chapter, I view the process of transformative learning through the lens of psychological type theory. I first describe Jung's theory, and then I go through the various aspects of transformation to see how they might be different for people with different psychological preferences. I do not wish to minimize or ignore the important differences in how Jung and Mezirow thought about the human psyche. I respect Dirkx's (Cranton & Dirkx, 2005) uneasiness about drafting psychological type theory onto Mezirow's transformative learning theory. Jung's work on individuation and other psychological processes was extrarational in nature. However, I believe his writing on psychological type theory can stand alone and be used to deepen our understanding of transformative learning.

Psychological Type Theory

The ideal and aim of science do not consist in giving the most exact description of the facts . . . but in establishing certain laws, which are merely abbreviated expressions for many diverse processes that are yet to be conceived to be somehow correlated. This aim goes beyond the purely empirical by means of the *concept*, which, though it may have general and proved validity, will always be a product of the subjective constellation of the investigator. . . . This well-known fact must nowhere be taken more seriously than in psychology. (Jung, 1971, pp. 8–9)

Jung argued that the observer in psychology must see both subjectively and objectively; he was highly critical of the idea that there can be objective psychology. Following constructivist thinking, Jung realized that the theorist who attempts to explain patterns in others is doing so through his or her own perspective. He commented frequently and powerfully on the difficulty in describing and interpreting psychological types. He repeatedly cautioned his readers against stereotyping and made a strong case against the quantification or measurement of psychological type preferences (because this runs the risk of objectifying the observation). Jung also was clear that psychological type was but one way of discussing human characteristics.

Introversion and Extraversion

Jung (1971) began the development of psychological type theory by recognizing introverted and extraverted attitudes. No one is entirely introverted or extraverted; these preferences are on a continuum. Unfortunately, popular literature overlooks this complexity (e.g., Cain, 2013). As a result, conversations about introversion and extraversion have become distorted.

Introversion is an inner orientation. The subject, the self, is more important than the object, the world outside of the self. A person with a tendency toward introversion views the world subjectively, in relation to himself or herself. In everyday language, we associate introversion with being quiet and shy, and this may be so, but it is not necessarily a characteristic of introversion. The distinguishing factor is the orientation to the self rather than to the outside world. When it is raining, the person who is more introverted interprets the rain in relation to how he or she feels about it—"It is raining, and I feel depressed when it rains" or "This scene reminds me of the time when I experienced one of the happiest occasions of my life." Responses to others, to events, and to readings tend to be personalized, related to the self.

Extraversion is an outward orientation. When demonstrating an extraverted attitude, a person tends to think, feel, and act in relation to the object, to the things in the world. Objects, people, and events in the world are often accepted rather than interpreted in relation to the self. Jung (1971) described it as a "ready acceptance of external happenings, a desire to influence and be influenced by events, a need to join in and get 'with it,' the capacity to endure bustle and noise of every kind, and actually find them enjoyable, constant attention to the surrounding world, the cultivation of friends and acquaintances" (p. 549). Jung (1971) went on in this description to say that people who are more extraverted are less discriminating in their selection of acquaintances, may be overly interested in how they present themselves, and have "a strong tendency to make a show of" (p. 549) themselves. I find it interesting to notice how Jung's language borders on reflecting distaste for extraversion; Jung was clearly on the introverted end of this continuum himself. The example in Box 5.1 indicates how a person with more extraversion and a person with more introversion may vary in responses to information. The extraverted attitude focuses on the external world as it is, and the more introverted attitude personalizes the information.

Box 5.1. Example of Introversion and Extraversion

Sam: "My uncle turned 101 last week!"

Pamela (more extraverted): "How wonderful! How is his health? Does he still live on his own?"

Arthur (more introverted): "I'll never live so long. The way I live, I'll be lucky to see 65."

Jung emphasized the importance of integrating the introverted and extraverted attitudes. Writing in the 1920s, he argued against the church and modern science, both of which he saw as favoring objective, empirically determined descriptions over the more subjective inner world. One of his missions was to establish the validity of the internal experiences of ideas, fantasy, and archetypes, which he saw as necessary for individuation and self-actualization. It is interesting to think about this in relation to the movement to bring the extrarational into transformative learning (see Chapter 3). Jung was making the same argument more than 90 years ago.

Functions

Jung was not satisfied with introversion and extraversion as a way of describing differences among people. It did not account well enough for the variations he observed. It took him another 10 years to formulate the now very familiar four psychological functions: thinking, feeling, sensing, and intuition.

Thinking and feeling became, in the final form of the theory, the two judgmental (or rational) functions. Use of the thinking function involves making judgments and decisions through logical analysis and problem solving. Use of the feeling function involves making judgments and decisions by considering values—one's own values and those of others.

Sensing and intuition are the two perceptive (or irrational) functions. Using the sensing function to perceive relies on gathering information through the senses—sight, touch, hearing, taste, and smell. Using the intuitive function to perceive relies on hunches, imagination, and fantasy; the perception occurs in an unconscious way. "The content presents itself whole and complete, without our being able to explain or discover how this content came into existence," said Jung (1971, p. 453).

Psychological Types

The combination of the two attitudes (introversion and extraversion) and the four functions (thinking, feeling, sensing, and intuition) yields eight psychological types. Some popular inventories, such as the Myers-Briggs Type Indicator (MBTI), come up with different combinations (16 types for the MBTI), but I choose to stay congruent with Jung's theory. I review each of the eight combinations of attitudes and functions with a cautionary note that no one has all of the characteristics of one type, nor are "types" independent of each other; people have characteristics of each type in varying strengths.

Extraverted Thinking

When thinking is extraverted, it focuses on the object outside of the self, the external world. Using information from the external world, a person who prefers extraverted thinking applies logical and analytical processes to solve problems and make judgments. He or she aims to establish order in life and is more interested in facts and ideas than other people. The person may appear to be impersonal or unfriendly to others who are more people oriented.

People who prefer extraverted thinking usually expect others around them to adhere to their principles. They may assume the role of social or organizational reformer and are generally idealists. Their thinking is positive, productive, progressive, and creative. They are sure of themselves and their ideals and principles and will pursue these ideals in the face of any opposition.

Extraverted Feeling

Feeling is also a judgmental function; however, rather than using objective criteria, people who prefer this psychological type use traditional or generally accepted values (those external to the self) to make judgments. Jung (1971) put it well when he wrote, "I may feel moved, for instance to say that something is 'beautiful' or 'good,' not because I find it 'beautiful' or 'good' from my own subjective feeling about it, but because it is fitting and politic to call it so, since a contrary judgment would upset the general feeling situation" (p. 355).

Their reliance on generally accepted values leads people who prefer extraverted feeling to a desire for harmony in their surroundings—conflicts in values would upset their process of using values to determine their behavior. As a result, they easily adapt their own stance to match that expressed by others. They smooth over differences. People with this preference make friends easily, work well with others in groups, and are very pleasant to be with.

Extraverted Sensing
When a person's sensing function is focused on the world external to the self, he or she perceives the world as it is and accumulates experiences of reality with little interpretation or judgment. People with this preference are interested in tangible reality, are practical and down to earth, are not bothered by violations of logic, and are not much concerned about the relationships among the things they perceive or abstract and theoretical conceptualizations of the world.

Individuals who prefer extraverted sensing enjoy things of the senses— good food, beautiful objects, and attractive people. The concrete facts and experiences they perceive with their senses provide the basis of what comes next. What happens once will happen again; what worked well last time will work well next time. Others see these individuals as good company and people who enjoy life.

Extraverted Intuition
When intuition is focused outward, unconscious perception is directed to external objects. Jung (1971) said this is manifested by "an attitude of expectancy, by vision and penetration" (p. 366). The intuitive function transmits images, leading the person who prefers this function to seek the possibilities inherent in every situation. Ordinary events hold great potential; every locked door needs to be opened.

People who prefer extraverted intuition are intensely interested in new situations, events, and objects; they approach them without judgment. They are likely to be initiators of new enterprises, champions of causes, and visionaries. They may appear to be indifferent to anything that is not a part of their vision and uninfluenced by thoughts or feelings, their own or others'. Sometimes, when the novelty of a new project wears off, people who are strongly extraverted and intuitive may lose interest and abandon the project. Other times, they may appear manipulative as they go about reforming some aspect of the world. However, their great enthusiasm and their ability to visualize possibilities draws others to their charisma and passion for change. An overview of the extraverted functions is found in Box 5.2.

Box 5.2. Overview of the Extraverted Functions

Situation: A work team has come to an impasse in preparing a marketing plan for electronic mosquito repellers.

Sheila (with a preference for extraverted thinking):

> Let's just get this done! Here, I've divided the job up into five parts. If we each take one part and bring it back tomorrow, I'll put it together.

Pat (with a preference for extraverted feeling):

> It's important that everyone feels involved in this decision. Let's just stop a minute and hear from each of the team members, find out what everyone would like to do.

Jim (with a preference for extraverted sensing):

> Why don't we just look up the marketing plan we had for the ant traps? That worked well. We can just follow that.

Robert (with a preference for extraverted intuition):

> Wait, wait. We need to consider the bigger picture. The environmental issues, the alternatives to electronic repellers—there's so much more to bring into this before we finalize the plan. Why, I think we could hook up with the Green Party.

Introverted Thinking

When thinking is focused inward, the criteria used for making judgments come from within the person, rather than from the external world, as they do when thinking is extraverted. Ideas have their origin not in objective data, but in subjective (of the self) thought. People who prefer introverted thinking are relatively uninfluenced by the thoughts and perceptions of other people. They enjoy working with theories and models and are less interested in the practical application of these theories. They like to formulate questions, gain new insights, and create new theories, often just for the sake of creating the theory.

The strength of individuals who prefer the introverted thinking function lies in the clarity, organization, and precision of their ideas, and less so in originality or their ability to persuade others of their ideas. They may only collect facts as evidence for their views and discard those that do not fit. They have strong inner principles by which they live, they are reflective, and they value truth. People with this preference need time to think things through as the judgment processes are internal. To other people, those who use introverted thinking may seem inconsiderate or even arrogant as they tend to judge others harshly when their ideas are not quickly embraced or appreciated.

Introverted Feeling

When the feeling function is inner oriented, judgments are made based on subjective, inner values rather than the traditional, accepted values important to extraverted feeling. Values are personalized; they come from within. Jung (1971) describes people who prefer introverted feeling as "mostly silent, inaccessible, and hard to understand" (p. 389). Because of the introverted focus, others simply do not see what is going on in that person. People with a preference for introverted feeling have an outward demeanor of harmony, but they may be inclined to melancholy. They prefer to live in a quiet, inner world of their own values, visions, and feelings. They have an inner intensity that others do not see, and they may be misunderstood as a result.

When individuals have a strong preference for introverted feeling, the outside world acts only as a stimulus; they are not much influenced by the actions or values of others. Although they most often choose not to express it, they possess a depth of feeling others usually cannot grasp. They enjoy solitude and have a strong sense of self-containment.

Introverted Sensing

When the sensing function is introverted, it is guided by the subjective sensation in reaction to an objective stimulus. In other words, the person who prefers introverted sensing may see the same object that another person sees, but he or she sees it in a subjective way—the object is personalized and special meaning is attached to it. The senses are used to gather information from the world, and that information is immediately made personal, related to the self.

An individual who prefers introverted sensing might, for example, collect paintings and be primarily interested in how those paintings reflect various facets of himself or herself. Or, looking at an object, the person might immediately respond in terms of a memory of a similar object or a personal association with the object ("That chair reminds me of the one my mother sat in when I was a child. That color is the color of the shirt I wore when I went for my first job interview."). If asked to describe the object, the person would give a representation of his or her impression of the object. People who have a strong introverted sensing function are more in tune with their own perceptions of reality than with those of others. They prefer quiet arrangements and routines. They enjoy taking care of the details of life and feel a sense of accomplishment when all of the little chores have been taken care of for the day. Their greatest strength is their sensitivity to people and objects, but others may see this as arbitrary and unpredictable as it is based on interpretation rather than reality.

Introverted Intuition

People who have a preference for introverted intuition are also stimulated by an external object; however, rather than encouraging attaching personal meaning to it as happens with the sensing function, the object prompts the person to release inner images and fantasies. Jung sees these inner images as being released from the unconscious. This person may look at a chair and imagine dozens of different ways in which chairs could be constructed or see the possible alternative uses for chairs. The images need not have any immediate utility (others may describe this as daydreaming), and they may be fleeting.

Individuals who strongly prefer introverted intuition may be those who come up with ideas on how things could be—they have unusual and imaginative ways of seeing the world. They often cannot connect these ideas to reality outside of the self, as their focus is inner oriented. They may be frequently misunderstood, described as mysterious, not able to reveal themselves to others, and seen as indifferent or even untruthful (because they are not connected to tangible reality). An overview of the introverted functions is found in Box 5.3.

Box 5.3. Overview of the Introverted Functions

Situation: Observing a painting at the Museum of Modern Art

Patricia (with a preference for introverted thinking):

> I like the symmetry of the lines and the use of blue and green to develop mood. But this yellow blotch over here doesn't seem to fit.

Tony (with a preference for introverted feeling):

> I feel calm and happy when I look at this. The blues and greens are calming, and the yellow represents happy sunshine for me.

(continues)

(continued)

Pamela (with a preference for introverted sensing):

> This really reminds me of the wallpaper that was in my parents' bedroom when I was a child. I always felt so comforted by that combination of colors.

Victor (with a preference for introverted intuition):

> I am reminded of the way blue symbolizes the unconscious, water, and the womb. I can see that there could be fish underneath that water, fish that are devouring each other in a battle to come to the exit from the womb.

Profiles

Now that I have taken the various facets of psychological type theory apart and described each one separately, it is important to put them back together again and understand this as an integrative, holistic way of seeing a person, not as a categorization system or a one-dimensional, stereotyping label. Even though Jung cautioned against quantifying psychological type preferences (and I agree with this caution), I think we can create useful descriptions of preferences if we maintain a holistic view. A colleague and I designed and validated such an approach to assessing psychological type preferences (Cranton & Knoop, 1995).

In the Personal Empowerment through Type (PET) check, each person receives a profile of preferences. First, most people prefer introversion or extraversion, even though they have both in their personality. Second, most people have a dominant or most preferred function—this is the function they are most comfortable using and the one they use naturally and often. Third, individuals have an auxiliary or secondary function that they use less often but with which they are still comfortable. Because everyone both perceives the world and makes judgments on it, the dominant and auxiliary functions cover both of these areas. For example, if thinking is my strongest preference, then I need an auxiliary function that is perceptive—either sensing or intuition. Fourth, people have an inferior function or a shadow side—the function they rarely use and do not understand. This function is mostly unconscious.

If the strength of each of the eight attitude-function combinations is assessed or described separately and then put together into a profile, a wealth of information can be obtained. Based on my experience in working with psychological type profiles, I give a few examples of the kinds of understandings we can reach:

- If a person's thinking and feeling functions are equal in strength on her extraverted side, but she has a stronger thinking function on her introverted side, she will have difficulty making judgments in the external world and will need to turn inward to use her thinking function.
- If a person's extraverted feeling function is strong and his introverted thinking function is equally strong, he will make judgments when he is inwardly oriented that do not seem to hold up when he takes them into the outside world.
- When all four judgmental functions (extraverted thinking and feeling, introverted thinking and feeling) are equally strong, the person will experience conflict and difficulty in making decisions and judgments.
- When the sensing and intuitive functions are equally strong, the person will flip back and forth between focusing on the tangible, here-and-now world and the possibilities for changing the world or seeing it in different ways.
- A person whose perceptive functions (sensing and intuition) are much stronger than her judgmental functions (thinking and feeling) will be reluctant to stop collecting information or envisioning possibilities and come to closure or to a decision.

There are many more combinations of preferences that could be discussed, but my goal here is to emphasize the complexity of psychological type profiles when they are viewed as a whole. Looking only at a person's dominant function or dominant and auxiliary functions limits us.

Differentiation

Some people, at different points in their lives, do not express clear preferences for one function over another. Jung related this to a concept he called *differentiation*: Jung explained,

> Differentiation means the development of differences, the separation of parts from a whole. . . . So long as a function is still so fused with one or more other functions—thinking with feeling, feeling with sensation, etc.— that it is unable to operate on its own, it is an *archaic* condition, i.e. not differentiated. (Jung, 1971, p. 424)

If we think of taking an average of many individuals, we could come up with an aggregate profile of preferences in which each of the functions would be of about the same strength. This would represent the collective of humanity but would tell us nothing about any one individual.

Jung saw the goal of psychological development as being to differentiate ourselves from the collective of humanity. How am I different? What makes me unique? Who am I really, as separate from another? When a person's psychological type profile is such that he or she has equal preferences for the functions, then it is as though this individual is one with the collective of humanity. That person has no unique pattern. It is as though he or she is trying to be everything that everyone is, unable to say, "I am like this, but I am not like that."

At the same time, Jung said that the conscious development of the psychological type functions is a lifelong goal. If a person deliberately chooses to develop other ways of being and becomes aware of and able to use different functions at different times, this is working toward a kind of wholeness or integration with humanity. The key here is consciousness. Unconscious undifferentiation makes for confusion between self and other, not knowing who the self is. Conscious development of psychological functions leads to the ability to be both different from and the same as others in a purposeful way.

Individuation

As I mention in Chapter 2, Jung's concept of individuation has now become an important way of understanding transformative learning theory. Jung (1971) said that individuation is "a process of *differentiation* having for its goal the development of the individual personality" (p. 448). Individuation is a transformative process, one in which we bring the unconscious into consciousness and develop a dialogue with that aspect of our self, come to a better understanding of our shadow, become aware of our animus or anima (masculine or feminine soul), realize the influence of archetypes, and learn to see how we engage in projection. Sharp (2001) described individuation as a circular odyssey or spiral, a journey where the aim is to get back to where you started, but knowing where you have been. We essentially remain who we are, but through the journey of individuation, we come to know who that self is.

In relation to psychological type theory, one aspect of individuation is the clarification of psychological preferences—developing a clear profile of preferences—which can then, in turn, be consciously developed. In transformative learning theory, psychological preferences are one type of habit of mind on which we may engage in critical questioning. Mezirow (2012) acknowledged this as a psychological meaning perspective. At the same time, our preferences influence how we engage in that questioning. And to go one step further, clarifying and developing preferences through the lifelong journey of individuation is transformative. In the remainder of this chapter,

I discuss how our psychological type preferences may influence the way we experience transformation.

Transformative Learning and Psychological Type

Perhaps one of the reasons researchers and theorists have sought to expand Mezirow's (2000) conceptualization of transformative learning theory is that Mezirow's approach was one of reason, a process comfortable to individuals with a preference for the thinking function, but seen as limiting to someone who is more intuitive or has an inclination toward the feeling function. In this section of the chapter, I first go through the facets of transformation proposed by Mezirow and then turn to some of the elaborations on his theory.

Reaction to a Disorienting Event

I am sometimes astonished by the experiences that my students are going through. They write or call me to tell of family tragedies and personal crises. Sometimes they contact me to say that they will be late with completing an activity; other times they say they will have to drop out of the course entirely and come back to it later. Whether it is a life crisis or hearing a point of view different from one's own, people respond in different ways to potentially disorienting events. This has to do with the content of the event, the circumstances under which it is encountered, and the place where a person is in life; however, I think it also has to do with psychological type preferences. People with a preference for the feeling function would seem to be those who would be most sensitive to encountering values different from their own. They are in tune with their environment and the reactions of others. Wanting to maintain that relationship, they are likely to be responsive to social norms, the opinions and questions of others, and issues in the media.

Those individuals who have a preference for thinking, on the other hand, whether the thinking is introverted or extraverted, have strong principles and points of view that are not easily shaken. An alternative viewpoint is likely to be dismissed without a second thought unless it is accompanied by a logical and convincing argument. Even then, the person may be more likely to respond with a counterargument than to question his or her own assumptions. I also suspect that in the face of more traumatic disorienting events, a person who prefers the thinking function is likely to cling to strong principles in order to get through the situation.

People who prefer sensing or intuition would be sensitive to disorienting events, but in different ways. Intuitive people are likely to respond enthusiastically to the possibilities and opportunities for change—losing a job opens up the possibility of many other jobs. When the sensing function is dominant, the person relies on routines and things happening as they have happened before, so it seems reasonable to expect that he or she would be shaken by an unexpected turn of events.

Critical Reflection and Critical Self-Reflection

Critical reflection—critically questioning the values, assumptions, and perspectives presented in the world—is the purview of extraverted thinking. This is what it means to use the extraverted thinking function. Coming up with alternative points of view would be a natural process for someone with strong extraverted intuition, but the reflective part would be less pronounced unless that person had thinking as an auxiliary function. A person who has extraverted thinking as a dominant function and extraverted intuition as a secondary function would be well suited to critical reflection, and a person who prefers introverted thinking would likely readily engage in critical *self*-reflection. People who prefer feeling may adapt rather than question, and those who have a strong extraverted sensing function may focus on comparing the current experience with a past experience in order to solve the problem (this may look like reflection to an observer, but it is a different psychological process).

Undergoing self-examination and conducting a critical assessment of internalized assumptions should come more easily to people who tend toward introversion, especially introverted thinking. All introverted types have an inner focus and, in a sense, are interested in exploring their sense of self. Whether the process could be called "reflection" for those who are going by feeling, sensing, or intuition is, however, debatable. Introspection, yes; reflection, perhaps not. But for those people whose thinking is inner directed, this activity is a natural part of their being.

People who have a strong tendency toward the extraverted side would have difficulty with self-reflection unless they deliberately moved to the introverted part of their psychological profile. This can be encouraged through activities such as journal writing or meditation, but such activities do not come easily to many extraverted people.

Discourse

Mezirow (1991) argued that participation in critical discourse is essential to transformative learning. "We all depend on consensual validation to establish the meaning of our assertions, especially in the communicative domain of learning, and . . . an ideal set of conditions for participation in critical discourse is implicit in the very nature of human communication" (p. 198). He reiterated this point of view when he examined the nature of reasoning within the context of discourse (Mezirow, 2003a).

Although this point of view can be contested (perhaps we need to understand each other but not necessarily agree), if we stay with Mezirow's definition of *discourse*—one based on Habermas's notion that rationality is inherent in the use of language—then it would again be those learners who have a preference for thinking, especially extraverted thinking, who would find this a natural process.

Mezirow (2003b) did go on to say that having an open mind, listening empathetically, bracketing premature judgment, seeking common ground, and having the qualities of emotional intelligence are assets for participating in discourse. Some of these characteristics go with intuition (having an open mind, avoiding premature judgment) and others with the feeling function (listening empathetically, seeking common ground).

People who are strongly introverted may find discourse hard. It takes time for stimuli from the external world to be processed internally (introversion). Introverted people often report that by the time they have formulated a response, the dialogue has moved on to another topic. Online discourse overcomes this obstacle (Cranton, 2010) but may introduce others.

Revision of Habits of Mind

Engaging in critical reflection and participating in rational discourse do not guarantee transformative learning. It is the revision of a habit of mind that makes the experience transformative. Sometimes people question, reflect, and discuss, but do not experience any fundamental changes as a result of this process. This may be a function of culture, society, family, or the workplace, but it may also be a function of psychological and learning preferences.

Individuals who have a preference for extraverted thinking may prefer not to revise habits of mind because they have a deep urge to stand by their principles and "truths." Those who are more introverted in their thinking may reluctantly revise perspectives based on new knowledge or an awareness of flaws in logic, but may not want to consider others' values or opinions in this process.

Following psychological type theory, it would seem that people who prefer the feeling function would readily revise their habits of mind—not through a process of critical reflection, but through a need to be in harmony with others' values. For a person with this preference, this is not a simple chameleon-like adaptation to others' views; it is a genuine shift in order to be at one with another. When feeling is more introverted, a subjective interpretation of the world is central, and perspective transformation would be an intense inner process.

When a person has sensing as a dominant function of living, either extraverted or introverted, the revision of a habit of mind would be most likely to occur as a result of immersion into a different situation, one that provides completely fresh sensations such as a change in environment or culture. It is difficult to understand the intuitive mind in the context of this rational approach to transformation of habits of mind. I suspect that the extrarational approach to transformative learning better describes the experience of an individual with this preference.

Extrarational Transformative Learning

Jung's (1971) view of psychological processes such as individuation is fundamentally extrarational in nature. We do not consciously choose one or the other, and we cannot develop inferior functions through critical reflection. At the core of individuation is establishing and maintaining a dialogue with the unconscious dimensions of the self, and this is not rational reflection as Mezirow described it.

Theorists as well as learners have different ways of seeing the world. The extrarational approach to transformation is based on an intuitive and imaginative understanding of learning and change. It transcends rationality and gives power and deep meaning to the connection between the self and the world. It nurtures the soul; it pays attention to the emotional and spiritual aspects of everyday occurrences.

It seems clear that individuals who have a preference for intuition, extraverted and introverted, would be more likely to experience transformative learning in an extrarational way. Perhaps having a combination of intuition and feeling as preferred functions would bring a learner closest to experiencing transformation in the way that Dirkx (1997, 2000) described.

Relational Transformative Learning

In the relational or connected approach to transformative learning theory, people are seen as learning through cultivating relationships with others, developing integrative and holistic ways of seeing the world, understanding others' points of view (rather than debating them), listening emphathically, and nurturing and caring. Individuals who have a preference for the feeling function, especially extraverted feeling, would be more likely to experience transformation in this way. This preference leads people to choose harmony over conflict and values-based judgments over logical, analytical judgments.

Belenky and Stanton's (2000) description of connected knowers is helpful in this respect. The more connected knowers disagree, the more they try to understand how the other feels and the more they make an effort to enter into another's frame of mind. This could be the crux of the transformative experience—entering into another's frame of mind with empathy rather than critically questioning or challenging points of view as is at the heart of Mezirow's (2003b) perspective.

Summary

It is widely accepted in education at all levels from elementary school to higher education (including adult education) that learners have varying preferences and styles of learning. Jung's model of psychological types provides a comprehensive way of understanding individual differences. Jung described people as having different attitudes toward the world: The extraverted attitude entails direct interaction with people, events, situations, and information, and the introverted attitude allows for indirect stimulation from the world but mainly consists of subjective inner-oriented processes. Psychological type theory also incorporates two preferences in making judgments: The first preference is the use of logic (thinking) one entails, and the second preference is for the use of values (feeling). Finally, Jung described two ways of perceiving: first is through the reality of the senses, and second is through intuition. Everyone has attitudes and preferences of different strengths as well as dominant and auxiliary functions that work together in various ways.

The process of transformative learning varies among people who have different psychological type profiles. The components of transformative learning theory that I have examined include reaction to a disorienting event, critical reflection and critical self-reflection, discourse, and revision of habits of mind. The language of Mezirow's approach to transformative learning theory is most consistent with a preference for the psychological type function of thinking, but people with that preference may also be ones who are the most unwilling to let go of their deeply embedded principles and assumptions. I have briefly discussed two of the alternative approaches to transformative learning theory—extrarational transformation and relational transformation. Based on the theoretical descriptions, it seems that individuals with a preference for intuition would be more likely to engage in the imaginative, holistic, extrarational experience and those with a preference for feeling would go through a relational or connected transformation.

6

EDUCATOR ROLES

I t is not surprising that educators doubt, question, and revise their roles continually. The literature bombards us with all of the things we are supposed to be: experts, resource people, facilitators, counselors, mentors, models, reformers, and activists. We read that we should love our subject, share our enthusiasm and passion, be knowledgeable, consider learners' needs, organize and structure learning activities in a clear way, be good listeners, establish a supportive learning climate, motivate learners, use humor, challenge students' perspectives to encourage critical thinking, promote involvement, provide positive feedback, use learners as resources, and consider learning styles, to name just a few of the suggestions.

As the education literature becomes more sophisticated and complex, so do the demands on the practitioner. Gone are the easy and safe days of the simple humanist approach of setting up a comfortable learning environment and meeting the needs of learners. Now we learn that we need to unmask power, challenge ideologies, and racialize criticality (Brookfield, 2005). Furthermore, as is our topic here, we need to foster transformative learning, and we need to be aware of a variety of interpretations of transformative learning theory and understand how they apply to different individuals. E. W. Taylor (2009) listed the core elements of fostering transformative learning: considering individuals' experience, promoting critical reflection, engaging in dialogue, creating a holistic orientation, being aware of context, and establishing authentic relationships. No wonder practitioners whose attention and passion is focused on working with their learners begin to feel alienated by the critiques and demands of some of the literature.

In this chapter, I rely on the framework used in Chapter 1—technical, practical, and emancipatory knowledge—to discuss educator roles that promote the acquisition or construction of each kind of knowledge. As Mezirow (2012) suggested, transformative learning theory redefines Habermas's emancipatory domain as the transformative process that pertains to both instrumental and communicative learning. The teaching of technical skills can also be approached from a more emancipatory and transformative perspective. I then turn to the centrality of power issues in fostering transformative learning; because transformative learning is about gaining freedom from constraints, limited perspectives, and oppressive circumstances, it follows that helping people learn how to exercise power must be a part of our responsibilities as educators. Finally, I explore educator authenticity. If we believe in transformation as a primary goal of education, this view characterizes our relationships with students, with the content, and with the context. We need to understand ourselves: our values, preferences, and the significance of our experiences. Thinking about authenticity is part of thinking about transformative education.

Educator Roles and Technical Knowledge

There can be no doubt that our way of teaching depends in part on what we are teaching. The current adult and higher education literature places little emphasis on the acquisition of technical knowledge, but this is what many people do—help others learn technical knowledge and skills, especially in programs designed to help students enter and be prepared for taking a place in the workforce. In my summer school teaching where a good proportion of the participants were trade and technology instructors, people expressed great relief when I acknowledged the importance of their teaching in our society. I am also very conscious of how instrumental learning (the acquisition of technical knowledge) spirals into transformative learning and how, in turn, transformative learning can lead people to the further need for instrumental learning (Cranton, 2009). Learning how to be a carpenter has as much potential to lead people into a deep shift in the way they see themselves and the world around them as does studying critical theory or exploring childhood traumas through narrative.

Working with technical knowledge leads to certain educator roles. Although technical knowledge could be discovered or constructed, it would be a time-consuming and perhaps unnecessary endeavor. Those individuals who deny that any knowledge exists "out there" and promote relativism and constructivism as approaches to technical learning have probably not taught too many plumbing courses. I do not mean that critical thinking is not a part of working with technical knowledge; indeed it is. Students learn to critically examine and question techniques and diagnostic procedures, not accepting information at face value but recognizing a body of knowledge that is learned, practiced, and applied.

In this context, educators are *experts and authorities* in their subject area. Using Pratt and Collins's (2014) typology, they are mostly engaged in the transmission of knowledge. They are experienced and practiced tradespeople and technicians. The educator describes himself or herself as a mechanic, a botanist, or a physiotherapist. As an expert, he or she selects the content, orders it into an agenda or outline, selects materials and resources, and presents the content in a primarily instructor-centered fashion. Finally, it is usually the educator who decides when the students have mastered the content.

Educators who work with technical knowledge also often see themselves as *designers* of instruction. The educator considers the prior learning and experience of the learners, writes objectives for the instruction, arranges the topics in a sequence to progress learning from one level to another, designs strategies that are appropriate for the learning, and constructs evaluative techniques. In other words, a traditional instructional design model is followed.

Typically, instruction in technical knowledge follows a sequence in which information is presented, demonstrations of the application of the knowledge are given, and learners have the opportunity for extended practice. In some subject areas, problem solving or problem-based learning are commonly used methods. Learning is often hands on or experiential in nature. Critical thinking is often encouraged via questioning procedures, troubleshooting, and finding alternative ways of accomplishing the same task. In this way, the educator is also engaged in an apprenticeship (Pratt & Collins, 2014). That is, he or she is a skilled practitioner in the subject area, able to reveal the inner workings of a skilled performance, and make that performance accessible to learners.

We do not usually think of technical knowledge as the basis for transformative learning, but it seems that it has as much potential to lead to a transformative experience as does learning in any domain. My mother, who grew up in the city of Amsterdam in the 1930s, had no opportunity or need to learn to drive a car, but when she was later living in a remote, rural area of Alberta where the nearest neighbor was two miles away and her husband was out in the grain fields all day, her life was constrained and controlled by her inability to go anywhere. She never did have the courage to try to learn to drive, but I often think of the transformative potential that set of technical skills would have had for her. When I acquired the technical ability to make good photographs, the way I saw the world was changed. When people learn the fundamental, technical competencies of reading and writing, they often experience their more ready access to information as powerful and liberating.

Though the acquisition of technical knowledge is not necessarily transformative in itself, I see it has having the potential to provide a foundation for transformation. In my many years of teaching tradespeople who were making the transition to becoming teachers of their trades (Cranton, 2009), I witnessed many of these students who learned a technical skill related to teaching (e.g., developing a PowerPoint presentation) and felt that this skill made them feel like "real teachers." Their perception of their identity was changed.

Educator Roles and Communicative Knowledge

When the learning goals are for students to construct knowledge about themselves, others, and social norms, the primary educator role is one of *facilitator* of a learner-directed or a codirected (teacher and learner) process. The facilitator responds to the needs of the learners, fosters a meaningful group process, provides support and encouragement, builds a trusting relationship with learners, helps to challenge people's assumptions and beliefs, and accepts and respects learners. Brookfield and Preskill (1999) emphasized how the facilitator of discussion can, among other things,

- Help students explore a diversity of perspectives
- Increase students' awareness of and tolerance for ambiguity
- Help students recognize and investigate assumptions
- Encourage attentive, respectful listening
- Develop appreciation for differences
- Show respect for students' voices and experiences
- Affirm students as co-creators of knowledge
- Develop habits of collaborative learning
- Lead to transformation (pp. 22–23)

Vella (2002) made similar points in her 12 principles of dialogue education. She underlined the importance of relationships between teacher and learner and among learners, respect for learners as decision makers, teamwork and group work, and learner engagement.

In Pratt and Collins's (2014) typology, the educator is working within a developmental perspective and a nurturing perspective. In the developmental perspective, teaching is planned and conducted while taking the learner's point of view, so that the instruction can help learners develop increasingly complex ways of understanding the subject area. In the nurturing perspective, the emphasis is on creating an environment where students know that they can succeed but, at the same time, challenging them to do their best work.

In communicative learning, the educator often acts as a *resource person* and *manager*. The educator assists the learning process by referring people to materials, readings, experiences, or other individuals. He or she might also arrange visits to a field site and organize special events.

Because communicative knowledge is usually co-constructed with educator and learners, a teacher may become a *mentor* or a *model*. The model role is more common when the educator-learner interaction occurs in the workplace and the learner identifies with attributes and job functions of the educator (Pratt and Collins's apprenticeship model). The mentor role may be more likely in longer-term interactions. Mentoring is fostered by a relationship that encourages trust, openness, personal disclosure, and closeness (Pratt and Collins's nurturing perspective). The model or mentor displays a love for the subject area, expresses contagious enthusiasm, encourages personal interactions, and is open and authentic.

Because communicative knowledge is concerned with how we see ourselves and the social world that shapes us, the potential for it to become transformative (or emancipatory) is great. Our sociolinguistic habits of mind (see Chapter 2) are often called into question when we are exposed to new perspectives in the communicative domain. On an individual level, something as seemingly simple as returning to school after a prolonged absence can lead people to see themselves and others in a way that may be discrepant with their values and beliefs, which can, in turn, lead to transformation. This was the original basis for Mezirow's (1975, 1978) concept of perspective transformation. He became interested in the experiences of women returning to school when his wife, Edee, went back to college. Edee reported on the issues that her classmates discussed and her reactions to their stories. This led him to conduct research on women's reentry stories. The facilitator of communicative knowledge needs to be aware of this sort of transformative possibility.

Educator Roles and Emancipatory Learning

When the educator's goal is to set up an environment and learning context in which people critically question their habits of mind in order to become open to alternatives, it is emancipatory learning that he or she is fostering. Although the debate that began in 1991 when Mezirow wrote that "adult learning transforms meaning perspectives not society" (p. 208) continues today, there seems to be a stronger sense that transformative learning theory can be more holistic in nature and incorporate both individual perspective transformation and social transformation, without arguing about which must come first. The primary educator role for fostering emancipatory learning is that of *reformist*. The reformer sees education as a means of helping individuals and groups exercise their own power, which may result in personal and social change. This perspective aligns with Pratt and Collins's (2014) social reform point of view, in which the object of teaching is the collective rather than the individual. Teachers hope to introduce students to ideologies and texts that are embedded in their disciplines. Depending on one's philosophy of education, there are other, related roles that can be a part of encouraging emancipatory learning.

Freire (1970) described the educator's role in this perspective as being a *colearner*. He or she works with learners and tries to find out about their lives and experiences even as learners may be questioning their values. When this happens, students become coteachers, and knowledge is created collaboratively. For example, the educator working to increase literacy does not simply teach reading as a technical skill, nor does he assume that people will come to him when they are ready to learn to read; rather, he shares the experiences of the learners, learns about their culture and values, and works within that perspective toward his goal. Similarly, the group leader working in a women's shelter learns about the women's experiences as she works with them to question their views of those experiences. The educator who is a colearner is a participant in the process of learning—discovering, challenging, and changing. There is an atmosphere of mutual trust and respect, authenticity, and a sense of enthusiasm and interest in others as well as challenges of others' points of view.

The educator fostering emancipatory learning may also be a *provocateur*, one who challenges, stimulates, and provokes critical thinking. Brookfield is especially well known for his helpful writing on how to teach critical thinking. In his earlier book, *Developing Critical Thinkers,* Brookfield (1991) provided educators with a variety of strategies for stimulating critical thinking. More recently he has emphasized that this kind of teaching is inherently political in that it is intended to help people learn how to replace capitalism with democratic socialism (Brookfield, 2005). He then went on to frame transformative learning with critical theory and to view it as ideology critique (Brookfield, 2012; Brookfield & Holst, 2010). Teaching critical thinking is not and cannot be neutral—the point is to change the world. Teaching critically is as much about what we teach as it is a method.

The provocateur helps to ensure that the norms governing rational discourse are maintained as a goal and encourages the group support that is needed when learners experience challenges to their beliefs and values. The provocateur will guide students into an awareness of limiting habits of mind and help them deal with the discrepancies between their expressed values and their actions. Strategies for doing this are the topics of Chapters 7, 8, and 9.

Power

In the first edition of this book, I drew on literature from the late 1980s (e.g., Yukl, 1989) to understand how power is manifested in adult educator roles. From this perspective, position power is associated with the formal position a person occupies, and it consists of formal authority, control over resources and rewards, control over punishment, control over information, and ecological or environmental control. On the other hand, personal power has as its source expertise, friendship, loyalty, and charisma. It is partly based on the personal characteristics of the individual and partly on the relationship the individual develops with others. And finally, political power stems from control over decision processes, coalitions, co-optation, and institutionalization.

I still like the concept of position power and especially the distinction between position power and personal power. It is position power that creates a false and potentially destructive dynamic between educator and student. The educator conveys the message "I am Teacher, and so you will do as I say," and the student receives this message with anxiety and fear: "I must please this Teacher and do what she says." When I was teaching full-time in a face-to-face environment, I used to wander through the halls while the students were working together. I didn't have much to do, so I walked around and read the bulletin boards. I overheard the interactions among teachers and students in the nearby classrooms, which so often included sentences that began with "I want you to . . ." and were followed by some kind of directive. I do not mean to imply that teachers should not express their "wants," but when those wants are disguised as telling the students what to do, this is position power in action.

Perceptions of power have shifted in recent years as Foucault's (1980) ideas about power have been introduced into education, and perhaps especially because writers such as Brookfield (2001, 2005) have helped ordinary readers understand Foucault's work. The language has changed, but I think the ideas are mostly unchanged. In this section, I rely on Brookfield's translations of Foucault's analysis of power.

Foucault argued that sovereign power—that which is exercised from above by an authority, or position power as I called it earlier—has been replaced by disciplinary power in contemporary society. Disciplinary power is exercised by people "on themselves and others in their lives" (Brookfield, 2001, p. 1) and is based on knowing the inside of people's minds. The emphasis we place on individual achievement, autonomy, self-direction, learning arranged in discrete stages, and the fragmentation of curriculum is a demonstration of disciplinary power where people are sorted, classified, and differentiated. Power is omnipresent and is exercised continually in all details of everyday life. Disciplinary power exists in the way eye contact is made between teacher and student, how the message is conveyed as to who should speak, seating arrangements (including the common circle), and the form of speech that is considered acceptable. According to this view, power is exercised rather than possessed and is pervasive rather than held by an elite group and used to repress others. As such, it is impossible to "give it away."

Foucault presented the provocative idea that individuals discipline themselves—what he called self-surveillance. We watch ourselves because we want to stay close to the norm, to fit in, to be accepted and approved. This concept is based on Foucault's work in prisons. He described "compulsory visibility" in which a person can be watched by others but is never certain he or she is being watched at any one time. This is the case not only in prisons but also in modern society and institutions, where technology has led to a state in which everyone is visible in some sense with cameras recording their entrance into stores and banks, computers monitoring and recording their every transaction, marketing firms tracking purchases and preferences, and government departments keeping files on individual lives. We are never sure just when we are being watched, so it is better to behave as though we are being watched at every moment.

This is what students do, Brookfield (2005) argued. He drew on his own experience as a learner to illustrate how participating in what looks superficially like democratic, empowering discussion can be a competitive intellectual exercise in which students suspect they are supposed to speak frequently and brilliantly but do not quite know how to do so. Going back to position power, if students perceive their teacher as having position power—control that is based solely on his or her position as teacher—students will work hard to do what they think the teacher-in-power wants them to do.

Of course, discussion is not always a competitive intellectual exercise, nor is it necessarily perceived that way. Truly collaborative construction of knowledge certainly can occur. Our classrooms can be based on relationships of trust and respect, not fear, and power can increase power rather than oppress others. My goal here is to encourage educators to "unmask" or question their understanding of power and examine their practice carefully for ways in which power is hidden behind surface forms that appear to be free.

In spite of the seeming negativity of Foucault's analysis, his view was that power is pleasurable and productive (Brookfield, 2001). The exercise of power produces responses, forms knowledge, and informs discourse. One of the desirable effects it has is resistance, as it is through exploring resistance to power that we can understand what power relations are about. Where there is dominance, there is resistance to that dominance, and this helps us to see what we are doing and what it means to learners. If, for example, I set up a situation where students need to respond in a certain way and a certain number of times per class, it is likely that students will resist. This notifies me that I am exercising my position power in an unreasonable way, and if I am paying attention, I can modify my expectations and provide students with more choice, more autonomy, and more power over their own learning. So, unlike a situation where sovereign power (complete dominance with no possibility of resistance) reigns, our society's disciplinary power allows individual acts of opposition.

What does all of this tell us about power in the various educator roles I describe here? Brookfield (2001) reminded us that we can no longer divide educators into the "good guys (democratic adult educators who subvert dominant power through experiential, dialogic practices) and bad guys (behaviourally inclined trainers who reproduce dominant ideology and practices by forcing corporate agendas on adult learners)" (p. 22). We are used to thinking of the expert, authoritarian, or designer role as one in which the educator exercises power through making decisions about content, learning activities, and evaluation strategies. But the facilitator, whom we assume to be democratic and participatory, also uses strategies that embody disciplinary power.

For example, the inevitable discussion circle puts students under the surveillance of their peers; they are exposed and vulnerable, and their degree of participation is immediately noticeable. Learning journals and learning contracts allow educators "inside the heads" of learners and encourage self-surveillance as people try to write what they expect the teacher wants or, in other words, to stay close to the norm. They may even feel called upon to invent dramatic insights and experiences or to present ordinary experiences in an exaggerated way. In discussions, students feel obligated to live up to the (often implicit) idea of what constitutes "good discussion."

I recall an incident from my practice a few years ago. We were a small group, perhaps 12 students and a couple of facilitators. As often happens, there were a few participants who were quiet. We sat in the typical circle for our discussions. The discussions were lively and interesting; it did not concern me that a couple of people chose to listen rather than speak. But it did bother some members of the group. Each time we asked for formative feedback at the end of the day, one or two people mentioned the quiet ones. This feedback was distributed back to the group (surveillance power at its finest), but the speaking patterns did not change. The feedback grew more pointed—"You are depriving the group of your ideas and experiences," read one comment. Finally, a participant approached me privately and asked me to "do something" about "those people who won't talk." I explained that I preferred not to require anyone to speak, and he expressed strong sentiments to the contrary. They did not have the right to stay quiet, he argued; they owed the group their ideas. We did not resolve the issue between us, though I think it colored the process for everyone. The whole group was aware of the pressure from "someone" for others to speak. I am still not sure how this could have been managed so as to encourage or at least allow everyone to feel safe to contribute in the ways they wanted, without pressure to speak or exercise voice.

In the reformist or provocateur role of fostering emancipatory learning, surveillance power may be embodied in a different way. Brookfield (2001) suggested that "liberatory practices can actually work subtly to perpetuate existing power relations" and participatory approaches can "inadvertently reinforce the discriminatory practices they seek to challenge" (p. 22). One example that immediately comes to mind is the attempt to recognize women's learning and women's voices by labeling or stereotyping all women as relational learners. The intent is good, but the outcome is further marginalization. Even in a technique as simple as the critical incident, which is designed to help people articulate their underlying assumptions, people are called upon to make their "worst experiences" public—an example of the exercise of surveillance power (let me get inside your mind, and then I will "help" you). Becoming conscious of the power relations inherent in our daily practice as educators is essential.

Authenticity

In all of this talk about taking on specific roles, where does the teacher as a person come in? Can we just automatically become whatever we need to become in order to facilitate learning? I first became interested in authenticity in teaching through exploring psychological type theory (see Chapter 5) as a way of understanding students' learning preferences. If students vary in the way they prefer to learn, teachers surely vary just as much in the way they prefer to teach. I have long advocated that there is no best way of teaching—that we need to consider the nature of the knowledge with which we are working, the context of teaching, and the characteristics of our students. But I went on to think about teachers' psychological type preferences and began work on a book I initially called *No Bad Teachers*, a title that the publisher wisely discouraged. This eventually turned into *Becoming an Authentic Teacher in Higher Education* (Cranton, 2001).

Dissatisfied with armchair speculation about authenticity, a colleague and I conducted a three-year study of how educators describe authenticity and how they become authentic in their practice (Cranton & Carusetta, 2004a, 2004b). Interviews, observations of teaching, and focus group discussions with 22 educators led us to describe five facets of authenticity: self-awareness, awareness of others, relationships, context, and critical reflection.

Educators spoke about their awareness of themselves as people and as teachers, how they came to be a teacher and what that meant for them, their values, their passions, the conflicts they experienced between the realities of teaching and their values, and the ways in which they brought themselves as people into their practice. Teaching was a passion for many. They spoke of it as a calling or a vocation, as something that gave meaning to their lives.

Participants in the project recognized the importance of understanding others as a part of their authenticity. They showed a strong interest in and awareness of their students' characteristics, needs, and learning styles. Some educators also were aware of and concerned with students' personal problems and lives outside of the classroom, but others preferred to stay more distant.

The most commonly discussed facet of authenticity had to do with the relationship between teacher and student. This broadly included helping students learn, caring for students, engaging in dialogue, and being aware of exercising power. Part of this awareness is the ability to enjoy the expression of others' power. Educators talked about the nature of their relationships with students, and many project participants struggled with where the boundaries of their relationships should be, especially in light of their responsibilities for evaluation and grading. There was discussion of how open educators should be about their own lives in their interactions with students. Underlying many of our conversations was an intense and powerful sense of caring about students and their learning. We also found a variety of perceptions of how power contributed to or inhibited relationships between educators and students.

Being involved in relationships with others (colleagues, family, and friends) with whom they talked about teaching was also important to many participants. Being able to talk with others allowed them to maintain an integration of teaching, personal life, and the rest of their professional life— something they associated with being authentic.

The context within which educators work influences their perceptions of themselves, their students, and their relationships with students. Context consists of several levels: the content of the teaching; the discipline or subject area; the physical classroom including the size of the class and the room arrangement; the psychological environment within the learning group; the department in which people work and its norms and expectations; institutional norms and policies; and, finally, the general community or culture and the roles people expect educators to maintain.

Critical reflection was a strong theme throughout our conversations with the educators who participated in our project. Many used the term *reflection*, and there was a sense that people were critical of or questioning themselves, others, and social norms. At times, they were also relaying feelings, hunches, intuition, or insights from practice. Critical self-reflection and critical reflection on relationships with their students were the most common, but participants also considered student characteristics and the context of their teaching.

If we assume educator roles that are not congruent with our values, beliefs, and personality preferences, we are asking students to communicate with the role, not the person. Teaching is a specialized form of communication that has learning as its goal, and here our special interest is in transformative learning. The better the relationship among the people, the more meaningful the communication will be. In thinking about how authentic teaching relies on relating with students, I often think of a quote from Hollis (2001). He wrote, "The quality of all our relationships is a direct function of our relationship to ourselves" and believed that "the best thing we can do for our relationships with others . . . is to render our relationship to ourselves more conscious" (p. 13). Jarvis (1992) said it more directly: "Authentic action is to be found when individuals freely act in such a way that they try to foster the growth and development of each other's being" (p. 113). Similarly, Belenky, Bond, and Weinstock's (1997) work in developmental leadership illustrated this kind of inclusive, caring connection among people who are working hard to understand each other as they are rather than as they could or should be. Schapiro, Wasserman, and Gallegos (2012) addressed the "spaces and process for transformative learning in relationships" (p. 355). The authors proposed that transformative learning is the outcome of "our genuine dialogue with an 'other' or others" (p. 365).

In fostering transformative learning, we help to create conditions whereby students will become conscious of their assumptions, beliefs, and perspectives; realize that there are alternative points of view; and begin to see their perspectives in a different way. Many kinds of events can precipitate such a process, as I discuss in Chapters 7 through 9, but I suspect the authenticity of the educator contributes in an important way. Palmer (1998) has encouraged us to pay attention to developing our identity and integrity in all aspects of our practice. Becoming authentic is often transformative (Cranton & Carusetta, 2004a), as a person separates himself or herself from the collective norms. Authenticity in teaching not only helps to create honest and open relationships with students but but also serves as a model for learners working to define who they are.

Summary

Using the framework of technical, practical, and emancipatory knowledge, I discussed educator roles that promote the acquisition of each kind of knowledge from a transformative perspective. Educators who are helping students obtain technical or instrumental knowledge are most often experts and authorities in their subject area—people with years of practical experience and considerable theoretical expertise. They design the instruction by selecting the topics, arranging the best sequence of events, and choosing teaching and evaluation strategies that will best serve the learner. Although it might be possible for learners to discover or create knowledge themselves in this domain, it would not be practical or efficient in most cases. Technical knowledge often provides the basis for transformative learning in that it gives learners the skills and knowledge that free them from constraints, change their concept of themselves as people, and perhaps redefine their notion of work.

Communicative knowledge is constructed with the help of an educator as facilitator. Interactive methods, collaborative learning, dialogue, and group activities help students work through an understanding of themselves, others, and the social world they live in. When people create new personal and social knowledge, they often go on to question their preexisting perspectives and move toward transformative learning.

Emancipatory knowledge is fostered through a variety of reformist educator roles. Critical questioning, the presentation of diverse points of view, the examination of existing social norms, and the exploration of alternative and radical perspectives help students become more open in their views and free from the constraints of unquestioned assumptions.

Power relations are embodied in all of our teaching and learning interactions. In this chapter, I have relied on Brookfield's understanding of Foucault's work on disciplinary power and the subset of self-surveillance. Rather than giving away power, we need to learn to work with the power we and our learners exercise in all of the ordinary interactions of the classroom.

Finally, I turned and questioned the idea of educator roles by discussing the important role of authenticity in fostering transformative learning. Being an authentic educator involves having a good understanding of oneself and bringing that understanding into teaching, understanding and relating in a meaningful way with learners, being aware of the context of teaching, and engaging in critical reflection on practice. Authenticity not only brings us to better connections with students but also models the transformative process itself.

THE IMPORTANCE OF
POWER

The relationship between empowerment and transformative learning is an interesting and complex one. To some extent, learner empowerment is a prerequisite of transformative learning; at the same time, learner empowerment is also an outcome of transformative learning. Mezirow (2000) made the following comments:

> Fostering liberating conditions for making more autonomous and informed choices and developing a sense of self-empowerment is the cardinal goal of adult education. (p. 26)

> Adult educators create protected learning environments in which the conditions of social democracy necessary for transformative learning are fostered. This involves blocking out power relationships engendered in the structure of communication, including those traditionally existing between teachers and learners. (p. 31)

Through emancipatory knowledge, the learner is freed from the constraints of unquestioned or inflexible ways of knowing; the learner is empowered or perhaps enfranchised. However, transformative learning cannot take place simply because the educator or the learner decides that this is a goal of the learning experience. Engaging in the critical self-reflection that may lead to changes in a perspective is, in itself, a process that requires self-awareness, planning, skill, support, and discourse with others. Embedded in that list of requirements is a prerequisite that the learner already be empowered to some extent or at least be working in a context that is empowering and supportive.

As I discuss in Chapter 2, one of the ideal conditions of rational discourse is that the participants be free from coercion; another is that individuals have an equal opportunity to participate. If rational discourse is a key component of working toward transformative learning, as Mezirow suggested, then we can see that learner empowerment must accompany the entire process rather than be viewed as an outcome of a transformative experience. Even if discourse is not a necessary component of the process, it seems that the critical questioning of basic assumptions, values, and beliefs cannot easily take place when a person feels disempowered.

An illustration may be useful. Tracy has enrolled in her first course in an MEd program. She expects her teacher to tell her what to do, correct her work, and provide guidance for her learning. In Tracy's undergraduate experience, she could rely on her teachers to fulfill these roles. Her assumptions about authority are well developed and reinforced often. She is a parent who directs and protects her children. She turns to people in positions of authority when she needs help, especially her pastor. In her community, she respects people in positions of authority and is admired for doing so. In her world, social roles are clear.

On the first day of Tracy's new course, she meets an instructor who provides a detailed and frighteningly difficult-looking course outline. He reviews the criteria for evaluation in the course, emphasizing the importance of using the correct format for papers and how to cite articles. He advises students to buy a copy of the sixth edition of the American Psychological Association style manual, so they can start right away to use the proper writing and referencing conventions. He says that he assumes everyone has a personal computer and a high-speed Internet connection. Tracy thinks momentarily of her restricted budget and wonders how much a high-speed connection might cost, but then she returns her attention to the teacher, who is now explaining that learning to be a critical thinker is essential in an MEd program. "You are expected not only to read but also to be critical of what you read," he remarks. "Everyone needs to be able to sift through all of the information available these days, and not just accept things because they are in print or on the Internet." He goes on: "And you will be expected not only to be critical of others' work but also of your own work and your own thinking." The teacher discusses how they will work together as a group and emphasizes that everyone should feel completely free to interrupt him, ask questions, and express their views. He then gives his introductory lecture and, unfortunately, runs out of time, so the questions will have to wait until the next class.

This teacher—a composite of several teachers I have known—would say that he encourages learner empowerment. He uses interactive methods, he advocates critical thinking and critical self-reflection, and his classroom is democratic. Yet from Tracy's perspective, who already sees her teacher as an authority based on her own social norms, there is only confusion and anxiety.

This reminds me of a typical comment I receive in the formative feedback I routinely collect in my courses: "All of this self-directed stuff is fine, but imposed deadlines would be helpful." I have looked for different ways to respond to this genuine concern. Most recently, I have given students a week-long deadline, but what happened there is that they took the last day of the week to be the real deadline, and there we were with a deadline again. There's nothing wrong with deadlines; what is problematic is that I, as teacher, have the authority to impose deadlines. What educators think is empowering is not necessarily what learners think is empowering.

Unfortunately, as Brookfield (2000) said, the term *empowerment* has been used so often in so many contexts that it has lost its distinctive meaning; it is "far removed from the words and actions of Paulo Freire or Myles Horton" (p. 141). I take this caution to heart and attempt to use the term in accordance with its true meaning. In this chapter, I suggest we promote learner empowerment in at least four ways: (a) by becoming aware of power relations in our practice, (b) by exercising power in responsible and meaningful ways, (c) by empowering learners to exercise power through and in discourse, and (d) by encouraging learner decision making. Finally, I consider how individual differences among learners need to be considered in our understanding of power and empowerment.

Awareness of Power Relations

Brookfield (2001) suggested that we use the point of resistance to understand power as there are no power relations without resistance. An incident from a few years ago comes to mind when I think about what this means. I was facilitating a course on transformative learning in summer school. Students had the opportunity to design and lead various activities in the group if they wished to do so. I no longer remember the goal or the purpose of the activity led by this particular small group, but the activity itself stays clearly in my mind. Everyone had a name of a "famous character" taped on his or her back. Others could see the name, but the person who wore the sign did not know what it said. By asking questions of others, we were supposed to guess the name we wore. I asked many questions of many other participants, but I did not come close to guessing the name on my back. Finally, when I was the only one left (or maybe that is only my memory and perhaps there were a few left who could not guess), they told me the name was "Big Bird." To the great amusement of everyone in the room, I asked what "Big Bird" was. I grew up without television and have consciously avoided television and the television culture throughout my life. Of course, I knew it was only a game and the students were well intentioned and their laughter was affectionate, but I felt a sharp resistance to the activity and especially to the assumption made about all people having a knowledge of television. When one of the students leading the activity said, "We never dreamt that anyone wouldn't know who Big Bird was," I used the moment to talk about assumptions, but I can now understand this point of resistance as an entry into understanding power relations. I did not like it one bit that I felt foolish for not knowing a character that all children in North America know.

The student who commented that imposed deadlines would be helpful in my class was showing resistance. Students who complain that not everyone has a chance to speak show resistance. Students who object that they have a right to be quiet show resistance. The typical facilitator response to such feedback is to try to make a change to overcome the problem, and this is fine, but when learner empowerment is our goal, can we use these opportunities to increase our awareness of power relations? What is the student who wants imposed deadlines really asking? Perhaps it is an attempt to find out what the hidden social norms really are? If the student is engaging in self-surveillance and wants to be sure to fit in with the norms of the class, how can this be done if the deadline is not given? Surely it is not acceptable to do the learning plan six months from now? How about six weeks? Six days? How am I using power when I refuse to say what is a reasonable time for completing this work? This kind of analysis can help the educator and the learners to understand the power relations in the group.

In this same class, we talked about the discussion circle and questioned the assumption that it automatically promotes democratic interactions. In the days following that dialogue, students often pointed out ways in which the circle made them feel empowered or disempowered. Awareness of the issue led the way.

Brookfield (2001) suggested that "discussion as a way of learning that is quintessentially adult can be experienced by learners as performance theatre, a situation in which their acting is carefully watched" (p. 21). The unexpressed norms for good discussion are assumed to be known by the discussion leader, and participants monitor their own behavior and scan the environment for clues as to how they are being received. The facilitator participates in this by nodding, smiling, and somehow indicating what good discussion performance is. If the development of discussion norms was done by the group in an open way, perhaps self-surveillance and second guessing could be reduced. Making norms explicit and clarifying the responsibility of the group applies to more than just discussion. If we pay attention to resistance, we may be able to see the power issue on the flip side of the coin each time.

Educators who have learner empowerment as a goal should be conscious of the power relations implicit in the strategies we have assumed to be power free. Learning journals, learning contracts, self-evaluations, and collaborative work do embody disciplinary power. This is not to say we should consider abandoning such methods but rather that we need to become conscious of how power is exercised within our practice. Learning journals give the educator access to what is going on in the minds and hearts of students, a particularly insidious form of disciplinary power as it comes disguised as a legitimate academic exercise. Learning contracts require students to predict what they will learn and what it is worth, and self-evaluation may promote the feeling among students that they need to guess what their teacher thinks of them. Collaborative work also has the potential to put students into the position of feeling that they are competing with each other to gain the teacher's attention.

In exploring power, we also need to consider its irrational dimensions. As Sharp (2001) said, "People generally confuse self-knowledge with knowledge of their ego-personalities" (p. 89). Our power relationships often stem from our inner interests—unconscious fears, morally inferior wishes and motives, and childish fantasies and resentments. I sometimes become aware, for example, of a childish and rather desperate need to be liked as I am facilitating a group—a desire emerging from my shadow side. Issues of classroom control and management may have less to do with consciously creating an environment for learning and more to do with our unconscious need to be in control and in charge. Helping learners feel empowered requires educators to understand their own relationship with power, and this process is not always conscious or accessible through critical self-reflection. We may need to come face-to-face with our fears and vulnerabilities in order to explore how we use and experience power.

Exercising Power Responsibly

Some manifestations of sovereign power (exercised from above by a clear authority figure) are obvious and are usually avoided or rejected by educators—for example, talking down to students; allowing no interruptions or questions; and maintaining complete control over resources, information, and rewards. Nevertheless, this is not quite as straightforward as it appears. Teachers are perceived to have a role of authority in most social groups; it is the authority that comes automatically from holding the position of teacher that is the most troublesome here. I am not advocating that educators are able to or should give up power, for this is not possible, but I do think that we need to do our best to ensure that others do not perceive us as exercising sovereign power when it is not our intent to do so. To this end, I draw on the material in the first edition of this book (Cranton, 1994) to make several suggestions for exercising power responsibly:

- Reduce the trappings of formal authority such as standing in front of the group and using a title.
- Avoid being in the position of providing all of the answers, having the right answers, making all decisions, and controlling everything that learners do.
- Ensure that access to resources is easily available by helping people use the Internet, library, and electronic library; do not be the only source of material and information.
- Lessen the disempowering effect of grading by using some combination of strategies such as learning contracts, self-evaluation, peer evaluation, and flexible learning projects.
- Involve students in controlling the learning environment—both the physical arrangement of the room and the group norms and activities.
- Remain open and explicit about all strategies; learners should know what the educator is doing and why.
- Acknowledge and use expertise as a source of power that builds credibility and trust and serves as a foundation for helping learners question assumptions.
- Develop open and authentic connections with students in which respect and loyalty are meaningful components of the power relations.

Foucault (1980) maintained that disciplinary power—that which is exercised by people on themselves and others—has replaced sovereign power in our society and is exercised continually in all interactions. Disciplinary power is based on knowing the insides of people's minds; it is not deliberately engineered. A normalizing gaze keeps people in line, behaving as they are supposed to behave according to the social norms of the community or, in this case, classroom. Learners watch themselves (self-surveillance) in order to be an acceptable part of the educational community. How can educators exercise disciplinary power responsibly?

Brookfield (2001, 2005) suggested that we expose the mechanisms of control, revealing and undermining power that is invisible and insidious. We cannot choose whether or not to exercise power, but we can seek out the manifestations of power and address them directly. We can talk to our learners about how power is exercised in discussions and learning activities. We can observe the ways in which we reward and shape the kind of participation we expect to see and then be open about that process. We can seek learners' help in recognizing and interpreting disciplinary power and self-surveillance. We can assist learners to recognize that they, too, are agents of power and have the capacity to subvert dominant power relations.

Empowerment Through Discourse

Although all theorists do not agree (see Chapter 3), Mezirow (2003b) saw discourse as central to transformative learning. *Discourse* is defined as "dialogue involving the assessment of beliefs, feelings, and values" (p. 59). Participants in discourse try on the perspectives of others and adapt communication to another person's perspective. Having an open mind, listening carefully and empathically, seeking common ground, and suspending judgment help learners to assess alternative beliefs as they participate in discourse. Equal participation and freedom from coercion are central if discourse is to serve as a vehicle for empowerment.

There is something disturbingly circular about this. Mezirow (2003b) clearly stated that the "hungry, desperate, sick, destitute, and intimidated . . . cannot participate fully and freely in discourse" (p. 60) and "the only alternatives to critical-dialectical discourse for assessing and choosing among beliefs are the appeal to tradition, an authority figure, or the use of force" (p. 60). If discourse is central to empowerment, but the disempowered cannot participate fully and freely in discourse, I wonder how empowerment occurs. Along with two colleagues, I considered this dilemma based on a research study in which we worked with literacy students and their educators (Wright, Cranton, & Quigley, 2007). We reported that literacy educators told dramatic and heartwarming stories about how their students engaged in transformative learning in spite of being "disempowered" according to Mezirow's definition.

Mezirow went on to say that two capabilities are indispensable to learning to participate in discourse—the capability of critical self-reflective thought as described by Kegan (2000) and the capability of reflective judgment (the assessment of assumptions and expectations supporting beliefs, values, and feelings). The highest stage of reflective judgment (King & Kitchener, 1994) is one in which individuals engage in abstract thinking about and critiquing of their own as well as others' perspectives. Research associates these capabilities with age and education, with only college graduates reaching the highest stage of reflective judgment (considered indispensable to participation in discourse).

My concern is that this way of understanding transformative learning seems to be exclusive. Mezirow (2003b) did say that "overcoming the threat of exclusion constitutes a significant epistemological rationale for adult educators to commit themselves to economic, cultural, and social action initiatives" (p. 60), but, I worry about the individuals with whom so many of us work in labor education, literacy education, social services, and so forth. If we follow this particular line of Mezirow's thinking, the practice of educators such as Moses Coady, Myles Horton, and Paulo Freire would not have led to transformative experiences. The alternative theoretical perspectives in Chapter 3 allow us to step around the problem by minimizing the role of rational discourse, but I would like to maintain that we can keep discourse (or perhaps dialogue) and still engage all who are ready and willing to be engaged.

Some possible strategies for encouraging equal participation in discourse follow; their appropriateness depends on the context of the interaction.

- Find provocative ways to stimulate dialogue from different perspectives—controversial statements, readings from contradictory points of view, or structured group activities that lead people to see alternatives.
- Develop discourse procedures within the group. In order to meet its goal of validity testing, discourse needs to stay focused. Group members can be encouraged to take on the roles of checking and controlling the direction of the discourse, ensuring equal participation, and watching out for coercion and persuasion.
- Avoid making dismissive statements or definitive summaries. To minimize the role of disciplinary power and self-surveillance, the educator must be careful not to shape the discussion through implicit regulatory functions.
- Be conscious of nonverbal communication such as smiles, nods, and eye contact that can give clues as to what the educator is approving.
- Encourage quiet time for reflection within any exchange.

Learner Decision Making

The notion that students should have control over decisions to do with their learning has been with us for some time, but it remains a complex issue. Learner empowerment in an environment where the learner is told what how, and by when to learn seems unlikely. The early adult educators, who, often had a social action agenda, helped people set up learning environments and provided resources and guidance, but they did not determine the content and purpose of the educational process. In the 1960s, educational researchers examined what they then called "learner control," comparing it to traditional teacher-controlled conditions (e.g., Campbell, 1964). In retrospect this was a misguided application of experimental research in that no characteristics of either teachers or learners were considered, but it is interesting that such research took place at all. In the 1970s, in a time when instructional design models formed the backbone of curriculum planning, learner control was applied to each of the components of the design process—diagnosing needs, setting objectives, sequencing and pacing, choosing methods and materials, and evaluating progress. Knowles's (1975) approach to self-directed learning followed the instructional design model of that time, and although he added the use of learning contracts, the process was essentially one of the student becoming a designer of his or her own instructional activities.

In the 1980s and early 1990s, self-directed learning was explored in a variety of ways—as a personal characteristic of learners; as a method of teaching; and, with Candy's (1991) book, a multidimensional construct. Based on an exhaustive review of the literature to that date, Candy identified four facets of self-directed learning:

1. Autonomy (a personal characteristic)
2. Self-management (making decisions about one's educational path)
3. Learner control (making decisions about learning within a formal setting)
4. Autodidaxy (self-initiated learning projects outside a formal setting)

Jarvis (1992) pointed out the paradox "that while the ideology of society is that people are free and autonomous, a great deal of human learning is other-directed and certainly other-controlled" (pp. 141–142).

In the last decade, critical theory has informed our practice, especially in adult education. Brookfield (2005) outlined the tasks of critical theory:

- *Challenging ideology,* where ideologies are embedded in our language, social norms, and cultural expectations, and are reified—they appear as givens and, as such, are difficult to dig out and examine
- *Confronting hegemony,* with hegemony describing those things we have accepted as natural and commonsensical but that actually work against our best interests and in the interests of those who wish to retain control or protect the status quo
- *Unmasking power,* specifically using Foucault's concepts of disciplinary power and self-surveillance
- *Overcoming alienation,* where alienation is a product of living in a way that is incongruent with who we are, when we commodify ourselves and act as automatons

- *Learning liberation*, where, calling on Marcuse's (1978) concept of one-dimensional thought, Brookfield explained how autonomous thinking leads to critiquing the systems that manipulate us
- *Reclaiming reason*, the process by which we understand how preconscious, taken-for-granted perceptions determine how we experience reality
- *Practicing democracy*

Each of these tasks is relevant to students' involvement in decision making about their learning, but it is the idea of one-dimensional learning that seems to me to best explain the seeming paradox of learners wanting freedom and wanting to be told what to do. According to Brookfield (2005), Marcuse believed that we "learn our own servitude and that we have learned to love our condition of oppression . . . [as a result of being] lulled into stupefaction by the possession of consumer goods" (p. 188). We have been manipulated to feel happy, and if we knew it, we would want to liberate ourselves. It is one-dimensional thought that is the mechanism of control. One-dimensional thought is focused on how to make the current system better rather than to critique that system. Divergent thinking is discouraged; we are indoctrinated to not question and to stay in the existing framework. Marcuse suggested a way out of this—autonomous thinking. In order to promote this concept, distance through privacy is advocated (so that we are not continually in contact with collective thought) as is interaction with art. Brookfield suggested that the only way to break free of one-dimensional thought is to "immerse adults fully and exclusively in a radically different perspective" (p. 215). Teaching critically, Brookfield proposed, is about not only how we teach, but also what we teach. It is inherently political, and the goal is change. I would emphasize that we need to teach the questioning of all systems to be sure not to move from one form of one-dimensional thinking to another form of one-dimensional thinking.

What does this mean in terms of practice? Depending on the learning context, learner decision making may be encouraged by several strategies (e.g., Cranton, 2014; Kucukaydin & Cranton, 2012):

- Using participatory planning in which students decide on some or all of the topics for a course, workshop, or other educational activity
- Encouraging learners to suggest additional topics or substitute topics, lead discussions, bring in resources, and otherwise participate in the ongoing development and modification of the sessions
- Providing choices of methods; for example, suggesting that a topic could be dealt with in groups or in a large discussion or setting up the option of online discussion for those who prefer it

- Giving students a decision-making model they can use as a guide to participatory planning and development or, alternatively, helping them develop such a model that is specific to the learning context
- Suggesting that learners select and develop criteria for evaluation activities
- Encouraging students to directly engage in self-evaluation where this is possible
- Regularly asking learners for their perceptions of the learning experience and sharing one's own perception
- Keeping the decision-making process open and explicit
- Setting up teams or individuals who are responsible for some part of the decision making such as setting the agenda, forming groups, and coming to closure

When learners make decisions or when some aspect of decision making has been delegated to the learner group, the educator cannot overturn the decisions arbitrarily. The educator, however, remains accountable. If a decision seems inappropriate, the educator can discuss the problem with the learners and the group can reconsider the decision together. An interesting example of this process occurred a few years ago. In a course called Introduction to Educational Research that I teach online, I asked the participants, after two weeks of introductory material, to select the remaining topics for the course. They worked in participatory planning groups for a week and reported back to the discussion forum. I followed the planning discussions but did not intervene unless I was asked a direct question. The results were initially worrisome. None of the groups suggested any of the research methodologies (phenomenology, action research, grounded theory, etc.) as topics. Instead, they expressed interest in how to read the research literature, how to critically analyze research, research ethics, applications of research in practice, and research issues of particular interest to their work as schoolteachers. How could I lead a course on research in education without including any of the research methods commonly used in educational research? As I discussed my concern with the group, I realized that, for them, it was important to read, understand, critique, and apply research, but they were not and had no intention of becoming researchers themselves, so the details of how to use the various methodologies were of less concern. They were interested in seeing examples of different kinds of research, and they felt they would become familiar with methodologies through illustration and critique, but their primary goal was to work with material that would be relevant to their practice.

I wrestled with this dilemma over the next few courses. I continued to find it problematic to reconcile my responsibilities to the program in which I teach and my need to respond to the learning interests of the students in my class. I decided to take my own advice and recognize my expertise power. I have taught some version of Introduction to Research since 1976 at several different universities. I do have expertise, which I can share with students. I now select the general topics for the course. Within that framework, I suggest weekly activities and discussions designed to connect the topic to participants' practice. The discussion often wanders off to related practice issues, and I encourage this through my responses to students' postings. I am hoping that I am now walking the fine line between control and the responsible exercise of power.

Considering Individual Differences

What is empowering for one person may not be for another. Even though I am very familiar with individual differences in learning styles and personality preferences, I am still surprised when I encounter this in a direct and personal way. For example, I recount when, just other day, I was meeting a colleague I had not seen for several years.

In anticipation of driving to meet her, I polished my favorite old car, an almost-antique 1993 Saab, and made sure to wash the dogs' nose slime from the windows. To my dismay, she said nothing about this car, which was, in my mind, quite beautiful and unusual. Perhaps this was because she is more intuitive in nature and does not pay attention to details, or perhaps she just knows nothing about cars. I thought about this incident in relation to how students respond to our efforts to create empowering conditions for learning. Just as some individuals feel empowered through involvement in a discussion circle whereas others feel exposed and vulnerable, we all respond to power relations and empowerment strategies in different ways. In Chapter 5, I used psychological type theory to understand individual differences; I continue with this framework here and in the remaining chapters.

There are two commonsensical yet important ways to consider individual differences as we think about learner empowerment. One is to help learners develop an awareness of their own learning styles, psychological types, values, and preferences. Understanding oneself is a component of critical self-reflection, so this serves two purposes—fostering self-awareness and empowering people to make decisions as to how they learn best. The second important strategy is for educators to develop an awareness of how learners vary in their preferences and to incorporate this awareness into everything we as educators do. This does not mean that we need to develop four or eight or even more ways of doing everything, but rather that we are conscious of the variety of responses to what we do and how the same act on our part can lead to completely different reactions.

Learner self-awareness can be fostered informally or more systematically using various inventories. Informally, a variety of activities can be used—values-based simulations, critical incidents, and role plays, for example—or simple discussion and questioning can help people become aware of their preferences. Most people know how they learn best and are interested in talking about it and sharing their experiences with others. Often the simple realization that there are others who share their inclinations for learning in a certain way is extremely helpful for students who might have felt alone or isolated in their preferences.

A variety of inventories can be used to measure psychological type and learning style preferences. The Myers-Briggs Type Indicator (Myers, 1980) may be the best known of the psychological type assessments. A colleague and I developed the Personal Empowerment through Type (PET) inventory (Cranton & Knoop, 1995), which yields a profile of preferences rather than a category or label. Stuckey, Taylor, and Cranton (2014) have created the Transformative Learning Survey, which assesses the outcomes and processes of transformative learning and produces bar graphs that describe 4 outcomes and 14 processes related to transformative learning. Among the learning styles inventories, Kolb's (1999) Learning Style Inventory remains popular in adult education. As with any such process, we must take care not to stereotype, label, or support people in using their learning preferences as a rationale for avoiding specific activities.

The educator who is conscious of individual differences will become aware of how this manifests itself in empowerment efforts. Trying to push an introverted learner to be "heard" in a discussion circle is disempowering, not empowering. Asking someone who is thoughtful and analytical to express deeply personal emotions may increase self-surveillance and even lead a student to invent things to please the teacher, but it will not feel empowering—quite the opposite. Refusing to provide structure or guidelines for a person who feels he needs this support, at least initially, will only exacerbate feelings of confusion and frustration. Encouraging someone who is extraverted and prefers to learn by doing to engage in quiet critical self-reflection or the contemplation of abstract and theoretical issues will similarly feel disempowering to the individual. This is not to say that we should continually deliberately match our techniques to the expressed preferences of the learner—challenging people to develop their learning styles in new ways is important—but when empowerment is our goal, we need to work with people's preferences, not against them.

Summary

Although learner empowerment is often described as an outcome of transformative learning, I have argued here that people who feel powerless are less likely to engage in critical self-reflection. Empowerment is important to being able to embark on a transformative journey. An individual who is insecure, lacking in confidence, anxious, or unsupported may not be able to overcome the emotional barriers to questioning values and assumptions without first learning to exercise his or her power in relation to the teacher and other participants.

Educators can support learner empowerment in many ways, most of which exist in the small, ordinary, everyday interactions of the teaching and learning environment. We need to become conscious of power relations, including those that exist in the types of interactions we normally associate with democratic practice. Points of resistance are the other side of the power relations coin. We can watch for and examine students' and our own resistance to see where the power issues reside.

Given that power is exercised in all human interactions, educators need to not only become aware of where and how power relations exist, but also exercise power responsibly. Sovereign power, that which is exercised from above by a person in a position of authority, is fairly easy to identify and avoid. Disciplinary power is less visible and more insidious, but educators can work to expose mechanisms of control and help adult learners recognize their own capacity to exercise power. So as not to lose sight of the good contributions of humanism in adult education, perhaps we can also name other power states: collaborative, empathetic, compassionate, shared, or just plain dancing.

Empowerment through discourse requires our careful attention. We must not fall into the trap of seeing discourse as an elitist endeavor that only the most articulate and educated of participants can enjoy. This is not the path to empowerment, at least not for those who are less articulate and have less formal education.

Learner decision making (self-direction, learner control, student autonomy) has a long history in adult education and may well be one of the central tenets of our practice, especially in the humanist and critical theory traditions. I have briefly reviewed the evolution of the concept and provided some practical suggestions for encouraging learner decision making as an empowering strategy.

It is essential that educators do not assume that all individual learners respond in the same way to empowering strategies. Individuals' values, learning styles, past experiences, and personality preferences contribute to how they will come to feel empowered and how they will respond to our efforts to help them on this journey.

8

FOSTERING CRITICAL
SELF-REFLECTION AND
SELF-AWARENESS

The educator who has created an environment conducive to learner empowerment has set the stage for working toward transformative learning, but this does not ensure that learners will engage in critical self-reflection or revise their habits of mind. There is no way that an educator (or anyone else) can ensure that transformative learning takes place. Learners must decide to undergo the process themselves; otherwise, we are venturing into indoctrination, manipulation, and coercion. In a now classic article, Daloz (1988) described how Gladys could not imagine, despite the efforts of Daloz, alternative ways of approaching her job responsibilities. More recently, Tennant (2012) pointed out that the concept of authenticity implies that there is an essential self that is not changeable. There is some aspect of self that constitutes who we are throughout our lifetimes. One way of addressing this problematic understanding of change is to consider how our "true human qualities can be distorted by social forces" (Tennant, 2012, p. 17). Once we discover the distortions, our "true human qualities" can be revealed. This is congruent with Mezirow's (1991) description of *distorted meaning perspectives* (later called *uncritically assimilated perspectives* by Cranton [2006]).

We do not leave the possibility of students engaging in critical self-reflection, increasing self-awareness, and potentially transforming perspectives to chance. It is our responsibility to help people articulate and examine beliefs and assumptions that have been previously assimilated without questioning, and there are many things we can do to foster this process. In the following two scenarios, the first educator helps Tammy to feel comfortable but does not, at least initially, create an environment that leads to critical questioning, whereas the second educator sets Martin to thinking about his life.

105

Tammy grew up in a remote rural area of Tennessee and was the first in her family to complete high school. I was her neighbor at that time, and I shared in her joy. Tammy talked about her dream of going to college and becoming a nursing assistant. Getting to the nearest college involved driving "over the mountain," a 45-minute trip in good weather, and a treacherous one in the sometimes icy winter conditions. Tammy took a job in a local furniture factory with the goal of saving enough money to buy a car so she could get to the college. A few months later, she was laid off from her job; in addition, her parents were not well, and as Tammy stayed home to care for her parents and younger brother, the dream of a car and college became distant.

A couple of years later, when Tammy's family moved to town to be closer to the medical services they needed, Tammy nervously decided to finally go to college. I was able to stay in touch with Tammy and, hopefully, provide some encouragement. She was assigned to an adviser, who suggested she take two courses—College Orientation and Life Skills—as a part of her initial studies. Right away, Tammy could see that college was no place for her. Everyone was younger, and the women all dressed so smartly; her southern accent sounded foreign even to her own ears. But in her very first classes, people were quite friendly and supportive; the teacher asked to be called by her first name. The students all sat in a circle and shared their fears. Because people could choose their own goals for the Life Skills course, Tammy chose to work on her accent, develop a study routine, and learn how to manage her time so that she could continue to help with her parents' care. It was not long at all before Tammy felt she was a part of the group and that she could succeed in college. I lost track of Tammy and am not sure how her experience developed from there, but it was clear her initial experiences did little to challenge her perspectives aside from her initial anxious response to being at college.

Martin grew up near a small town in southern Ontario's fruit-growing region. His father had immigrated to Canada when Martin was a baby and did what he knew best—he established a grape farm. Martin's father had never learned to read or write but did not consider this to be especially important for a farmer. His vines were the straightest, his pruning the neatest, and his harvest the best in the area. Martin knew he would take over the farm one day, so he quit school as soon as he could do so legally and worked full-time with his father. He married young, and he and his wife built their own house next to a stream at the back of the largest grape field.

Life changed when the price of grapes fell to a third of their former value and the cost of fuel, insecticides, and fungicides skyrocketed. Neighbors were selling out; some were ripping out the vines and creating horse pastures. Martin decided to get some training in a trade to supplement the farm income. He chose welding as that would also be a useful skill to have around the farm.

Martin was shocked to find out that he was required to take Life Skills and Communications. What did that have to do with welding? He had plenty of life skills already, whatever that meant. The Life Skills teacher turned out to be a woman who was younger than he was. She had everyone sit in a circle, call her by her first name (and she was a teacher!), and answer personal questions. Everyone had to tell his or her "life story" to someone else, and then the teacher asked rude questions about each story. "Why did you decide to do this?" "How do you think you'll be able to manage in school?" Everyone was uncomfortable. But Martin went home that afternoon wondering why he had never really considered finishing high school. What did education mean to him? Why was he just following in his father's footsteps? Couldn't a farmer also be a person who learned things? He and his wife spent the evening talking about what the teacher had asked and how it made Martin feel.

Uncomfortable questions can promote critical self-reflection if a learner is willing and ready to consider the questions. Martin's experience promoted immediate self-reflection; Tammy's experience, on the other hand, was one of total support and comfort, which may well have led her to change later, but did not do so initially. Any strategy that opens up new perspectives, challenges existing assumptions, or presents information from a different point of view has the potential to encourage reflection and transformation. In this chapter, I present several such strategies: questioning, consciousness-raising experiences, journals, experiential learning, critical incidents, and art-based activities.

Questioning

In their review of the first Conference on Transformative Learning, Wiessner and Mezirow (2000) listed "Using Questions and Narrative" (p. 337) as one of the practical themes arising out of the conference presentations. Questions are effective, they suggested, in establishing an environment where people can figure out things for themselves, and questioning develops a constructive process appropriate for fostering transformative learning. Through thinking about and responding to questions, new avenues for understanding and new ways of seeing things are opened up.

Many general guidelines for asking good questions are given in the adult education literature, such as the following suggestions:

- Be specific—relate questions to specific events and situations.
- Move from the particular to the general.
- Be conversational.

- Avoid echoing students' responses to a question.
- Use follow-up questions or probes to encourage more specific responses.
- Do not ask questions that can be responded to in a simplistic, "yes-no" way.
- Ask questions that draw on learners' experiences and interests in relation to the topic.

Elsewhere, I have developed a framework for asking questions in order to foster four types of learning: learning something new, elaborating on something known, transforming an assumption or belief, and transforming a broad perspective or worldview (Cranton, 2003). For the first two types of learning, I have roughly followed Bloom's taxonomy in advocating memory questions, personalizing questions, application questions, analyzing questions, integrative questions, and evaluative questions. For the second two types of learning, I have suggested content, process, premise, spiraling, and feeling questions. It is this latter set of questions that are relevant to fostering critical self-reflection and self-knowledge; I elaborate on these here. Content, process, and premise reflection are described more fully in Chapter 2. The following are not meant as questions to be asked of students but rather to serve as a way of thinking about self-reflection and critical self-reflection.

Content reflection questions serve to raise learner awareness of assumptions and beliefs. In personal or psychological development (regarding psychological habits of mind), content questions take the form "What do you know or believe about yourself?" The educator might ask, "What do you see as your skills in this area?" "What would you like to improve?" "What is your perception of yourself as a learner?" "What are your feelings about this decision?" or "What draws you to this area of study?"

On a social level (sociolinguistic habits of mind), content reflection questions take the generic form "What are the social norms in this context?" For example, the educator could ask, "What was the perception of this in your home community?" "What would be the feminist view on this issue?" "What views do the media present?" "What are politicians saying about this?" "What does the way we use language tell you about this area?" or "What would you say to this if you were the union leader?"

Content reflection can also be related to knowledge and the way we obtain knowledge (epistemic habits of mind), moral-ethical perspectives, philosophical views, and aesthetics (Mezirow, 2000). Educators can ask, for example, "What knowledge have you gained from your experience in this area?" "What does your conscience tell you?" "What religious or philosophical concepts inform your view?" or "What about this is beautiful?"

Process reflection questions address how a person has come to hold a certain perspective. If it is a problem being reflected on, process questions ask how the issue became a problem. Asking process questions helps learners find the source of an assumption or a belief; sometimes it is useful to ask people if they can recall a time when they did not hold a particular belief and then work forward from that time.

Examples of process reflection questions related to psychological habits of mind might include, "How did you come to see yourself this way?"; "How did you choose this career?"; "Can you recall how you came to hate statistics?"; "How long have numbers made you feel anxious?"; "Can you remember a time when you didn't feel this way?"; or "How was your view of yourself as a poor writer shaped?" Psychological beliefs are often uncritically assimilated in childhood, so process questions may be difficult to answer, and other strategies for fostering critical reflection may be needed.

In the sociolinguistic area, process questions have the goal of unearthing the source of social norms that have been absorbed without thought. Again, those norms absorbed in childhood can be quite hard to identify. Questions may take the form of "How did the community where you grew up influence that view?"; "How did your experiences in high school shape what you believe?"; "Has the media had an effect on what you believe?"; "How does advertising influence your buying habits?"; or "Can you remember when you first encountered this point of view?"

Process reflection questions can also be asked of epistemic perspectives, moral-ethical perspectives, philosophical views, and aesthetics—for example, "How did you come to the conclusion that this theory is valid?"; "Can you recall when you first adopted that stance?"; "What led you to see this as unethical?"; "How did you come to appreciate this style of photography?"; or "How did you decide this research is flawed?"

Premise reflection questions get at the very core of our belief systems. They encourage the examination of the foundations of perspectives. Questions take the form of "Why is this important in the first place?" or "Why should I care about this?" In the psychological arena, educators can ask, "Why does it matter that you are afraid of spiders?" or, perhaps, "What are the consequences of your fear of spiders? How does this limit or constrain your life?" Care needs to be taken when asking premise questions about deeply held personal points of view; thinking about such issues can be emotional and traumatic. If I ask, "Why is your self-image of concern to you?" I could be unknowingly poking at the scar over a serious wound.

Premise questions in the sociolinguistic domain are the essence of critical theory. Ideology critique (ways in which people recognize uncritically assimilated and unjust dominant ideologies or sociocultural distortions) is one of the four traditions of criticality (Brookfield, 2005). Ideologies are embedded in our languages, social norms, and cultural expectations. They are reified—they appear as givens and, as such, are difficult to dig out and examine. Hegemony is perpetuated through mass media images and messages as well as social and institutional expectations and norms. People learn to live by the dominant system of beliefs.

We can ask, "Why do you value hard work?" "Why is it relevant what your extended family thinks?"; "Why do you care about pleasing your boss?"; "Why do you associate freedom with war?"; or "Why do we believe that it is only through education that people can come to engage in critical reflection?"

In regard to epistemic, moral-ethical, philosophical, and aesthetic habits of mind, premise questions take the same form, but focus on a different kind of knowing. Educators could ask, "Why is that knowledge important?"; "Why do we need to know that?"; "Why does it matter if I behave ethically in that situation?"; "What does understanding a philosophical stance contribute to anything?"; "Why would we concern ourselves with the existence of God?"; or "Why is art important in a person's life?"

To incorporate the recent movements to a more holistic understanding of transformative learning, I have added so-called spiraling and feeling questions to the repertoire of critical questions we can consider using. *Spiraling questions* show how each part of what we know about who we are is related to every other thing we have learned and experienced.

Feeling questions ask about spirit and body and call for imaginative perception in understanding constraints. Carpenters and mechanics who are becoming teachers of carpentry and mechanics are changing everything about themselves, not just a cognitive perspective on their practice. Where do they put their pride in their working man's callused hands? What do they do with their feelings of superiority based on their being able to do physical tasks with ease? How do they deal with their friends' views of teachers as soft and lazy? How do they understand the sense of vocation that brought them to teaching?

Consciousness-Raising Experiences

Consciousness is a peculiar thing. It is an intermittent phenomenon. One-fifth or one-third or perhaps even one-half of human life is spent in an unconscious condition. The conscious mind moreover is characterized by a certain narrowness. It can hold only a few simultaneous contents at a given moment. All the rest is unconscious at the time, and we only get a sort of continuation or general understanding or awareness of a conscious world through the *succession* of conscious moments. . . . Consciousness is very much the product of perception and orientation in the *external* world. (Jung, 1968, pp. 6–8)

Consciousness-raising is breaking free from one-dimensional thought, understanding and unmasking power structures, recognizing hegemony, and critiquing social ideologies (Brookfield, 2005). Consciousness-raising occurs through exposure to different perspectives; acknowledgement of oppression; and critical, serious questioning of our own and others' beliefs. Through the writings of Freire (1970) and others, *consciousness-raising* has come to be associated with freedom from oppression; the term is also used in this way by feminist theorists. Individual or personal consciousness-raising as described by Jung can be seen to form the basis of freedom from social oppression.

In some situations, consciousness-raising is promoted by exposure to new information, knowledge, insights, or values, especially those that are discrepant with our currently held points of view. But more commonly associated with consciousness-raising is seeing familiar things from a different perspective, thereby increasing one's self-awareness regarding familiar things.

Most people are fairly firmly entrenched in familiar roles—as professionals, as persons, and as learners. What happens once, we expect to happen again. We develop habits of mind, habitual expectations, and we make meaning based on these habits. Experiences that shake up these habits encourage critical reflection and expand self-knowledge. There are many kinds of learning activities that have this potential: role plays, critical debates, case studies, simulations, games, and life histories, to name a few. Whatever leads people to see something from a different point of view can act as a consciousness-raising activity. Here I review a few such strategies.

Role play is one of the more common methods of helping others see things from a point of view outside of their normal perspective. There are many variations on how role plays can be conducted. Generally, the purpose and context of the role play is described, and participants receive a description of the part they will play—usually not a script, but enough information that dialogue can be improvised. It is best if learners and educator collaborate on the scenario for the role play and integrate ideas from their experience and practice. Role plays that are co-constructed with educator and are ideal. Some people are uncomfortable with role plays, and although it can be good to challenge such discomfort, it is sometimes best to suggest that these individuals act as observers or reactors. Observers can watch for indicators of underlying, unconscious assumptions at play.

In order for role playing to lead to consciousness-raising, debriefing is important. Participants should have the opportunity to discuss their experience fully, especially what it felt like to view the situation from an alternative perspective. Videotaping may be helpful in looking for discrepancies between perceptions and behaviors.

Some informal variations include the following:

- Reversing roles in a discussion and presenting ideas from the other person's point of view
- Reversing roles that are played in real life (e.g., a manager and a staff member, a union member and a manager)
- Participating in a discussion from the perspective of various authors or theorists

Consciousness-raising is initiated when the assumptions, values, and beliefs underlying the roles are made explicit and questioned.

Simulations can also be used to initiate awareness of alternative perspectives. Predesigned simulations are available from a variety of sources, but generally I find it more useful to create simulations related to the experiences of participants or the issues being addressed. In a graduate program at Foundations Institute, participants had chosen to spend time learning about organizational change. A cofacilitator and I developed a simulation in which organizational teams designed proposals for a change in organizational structure and presented them to the board of directors. We called on other colleagues to make up the board of directors and booked the boardroom in our building. Each team came in to make its presentation separately, and my colleagues, who became fully engaged in the roles they were playing, asked challenging questions of each team.

In a gerontology group, participants can simulate the loss of hearing, eyesight, or tactile sensation by using earplugs, semitransparent blindfolds, or gloves before engaging in some routine activity. In a hospitality staff development session, a simulation of a hotel reception area can be set up with participants acting as clients, hotel staff, and managers. Whenever possible, people should be encouraged to take part in a simulation in a way that puts them in a position or permits them to take a stance they would not normally experience. In most subject areas, it is possible to set up interesting simulations that will help to reveal values and beliefs and allow learners to see things from another point of view. As with any such strategy, it is important to leave a good amount of time for discussion and debriefing.

Just as narrative inquiry and self-study have gained popularity as research methodologies, *life story* and *autobiography* have become commonly used strategies for encouraging critical self-reflection and self-knowledge. Tyler and Swartz (2012) explored the relationship among storytelling, transformative learning, and complexity science. They told a "story about a story" (p. 457) to illustrate how storytelling intersects with transformative learning. Dominicé (2000) encouraged the use of oral and written educational biographies as a way of understanding learners' frames of reference or ways of thinking about the world, and how this architecture is embedded in cultural roots. Dominicé deliberately used the phrase *educational biography* as he saw a person's life history as an educational process. He suggested that a person both write and tell his or her story and present both formats to others in a small group. Group members interpret and reconstruct each other's biographies.

A few years ago, I attended a retreat in which Jo Tyler led a storytelling activity. It loosely followed Dominicé's approach. Jo asked us to consider a story about our practice, one that was important to us, one that we thought about often. I did so. Jo then asked us to work with a partner. I was sitting beside a colleague I had known and worked with for many years, so we agreed to be partners. One of us told her story to the other (partner). The partner listened but did not interrupt or comment. The partner then told the story back to the storyteller. Next, the storyteller told the story again, taking into account any insights she may have had while listening to her story being told by someone else. I told the story of Jim, one of my students who was a tradesperson in a program where he was learning to be a teacher of his trade. Jim was the "class clown," as a way of coping with his fears about being in a university setting. Later, Jim broke down in class and announced he could not do this; he could not be a teacher.

When I responded to my partner by telling my story again, I had a remarkable experience. I spoke from Jim's perspective. I even spoke in the Maritime dialect that Jim used. I could see the story as it must have seemed to Jim.

Life stories may also be focused on an aspect of learners' lives that is relevant to their area of study or interest. Johnson (2003) offered a model for integrating autobiography with any subject area. For example, I often encourage people to tell the story of how they became teachers or adult educators. When I taught in a master's of adult education program, we opened each new cohort group with a journey exercise where individuals drew and then described the journey that brought them to the program. In an English as a second language program, individuals could be asked to tell stories about their cultures; in retraining workshops, participants could be invited to share their life stories in relation to job choices and preferences. Most people enjoy telling stories and listening to others' stories. When the experiences of individuals in a group are diverse, the variety of perspectives in the stories naturally leads to awareness of alternatives and consciousness-raising. The educator should also actively draw out assumptions and values implicit in people's stories.

Journals

Journals and diaries have long been used as a means of self-expression. Writers, artists, philosophers, scientists, and researchers use journals to reflect on their life and work. Psychologists and psychoanalysts incorporate journal writing into their work with clients. Progoff (1992), who studied with Jung, has contributed extensively to the literature on journal writing. The Progoff journal process is presented at workshops and seminars across North America. He suggested a variety of formats and journal sections that may be helpful: a life history; a dialogue with a person from the writer's life or with a historical figure; a depth-dimension section containing metaphors, dreams, and images; or a life-study journal written from the perspective of another person.

Journals are now routinely used in a wide variety of subject areas and with different goals or purposes, ranging from a type of log or anecdotal record of what students have done through to creative scrapbooks and web-based blogs. In order to stimulate critical self-reflection and self-knowledge through journal writing, we need to emphasize the articulation of assumptions, thoughts, and feelings about issues and the consideration of alternatives. In my experience, the format or style of the journal does not matter a great deal; it seems to work best when people choose a format that they enjoy and find comfortable. However, I sometimes provide suggestions or guidelines, especially when students seem to feel at a loss as to how to start:

- Divide each journal page in half vertically and use one side of the page for observations and descriptions and the other side for thoughts, feelings, related experiences, or images provoked by the description.
- Be assured that journals will not be checked for grammar or writing style or graded or judged in any way.
- Explore specific themes related to the course or program, such as "My thoughts on career options" or "My role as a professional" or "Past experiences that have influenced me."
- Establish a routine for journal writing—a time of day, a place, a special kind of book in which thoughts are recorded.
- Experiment with various styles and contents, such as writing to someone using a letter format, recording dreams, working with poetry, or incorporating drawings with text.

As I mention in Chapter 7, journals can be seen as a manifestation of disciplinary power. They are a way for the educator to "see inside of the mind" of the learner. We need to be conscious of this. No matter what we say, reading a journal gives us access to the student's thoughts that we would not otherwise have. The process can lead to a situation where people write what they think the educator wants to hear or, worse, invent stories to demonstrate critical reflection or dramatic breakthroughs.

I suggest that no one should be required to write a journal, that no one should be required to give a journal to the educator, and that journals should never be graded by an educator. Some alternatives might include suggesting that students can write summaries of their journals or choose excerpts to share with the educator, instituting dialogue journals or blogs in which students write back and forth to each other, or having students evaluate their own learning through keeping a journal. When we have the opportunity to read and comment on students' journals, our comments should be challenging and provocative but not judgmental. We should never contradict how the learner sees himself or herself, but we can question the origin of those perceptions and the consequences of holding them. Content, process, and premise reflection questions are useful (see the earlier section in this chapter on critical questioning). When I read journals, I tend to write many more questions in the margins than comments in other formats, though I am also conscious of indicating sections that I find insightful, interesting, and well expressed.

Experiential Learning

Dewey's (1938) *Experience and Education* provided a strong foundation for the emphasis in adult education (and education in general) on experiential learning. Dewey (1933) also described reflection through rational problem solving. Reflective thought involves "active, persistent and careful consideration of any belief or supposed form of knowledge in the light of the grounds that support it and the further conclusion to which it tends" (p. 9). This sounds very much like what we hope for in encouraging critical reflection as a basis for transformative learning.

Kolb's (1984) experiential learning model is another historical marker of the importance of experience in learning. He described learners as going through a cycle of concrete experience, reflection on that experience, abstract conceptualization, and application of the insights in a new context. Although people usually have a preference for one or more stages of the cycle, Kolb sees the complete cycle as comprising meaningful learning experiences.

MacKeracher (2012) wrote about the role of experience in transformative learning. She used a case study format based on her own transformative learning process. She started with three definitions of *experience*: "everything that happens to you between birth and death" (p. 343), experience based on events imposed by a cultural and social heritage (values, beliefs, and expectations), and constructed knowledge and the process of developing it (procedural knowledge). MacKeracher's case study included "learning that I was a teacher" (p. 344), learning to be a self-directed learner, learning to be a professor, and learning to be retired.

In an online course on transformative learning that I taught a few years ago, participants were discussing the transformative potential of moving from one culture to another and experiencing a very different lifestyle. It is often a new experience or new personal living arrangement that provokes the critical self-reflection that is a part of transformation. From the educator's perspective, there are innumerable ways to provide provocative experiences for learners, experiences that will challenge their ways of seeing themselves or issues in the world around them. Practicums in professional education (nursing, teaching, dentistry, social work) and apprenticeships in the trades (carpentry, welding, auto mechanics, refrigeration) have long been used to help people come to see themselves in a new way—as a teacher, carpenter, and so on. On a smaller scale, any venture into the real world related to the area of study can be an eye-opening experience (e.g., a visit to or volunteer work in an adult education center, attendance at or participation in the theatre, a day spent working at a farm, participation in committees). The emphasis on service-learning and job shadowing demonstrates how educators in many fields are recognizing the importance of experiential activities.

Although the experience may, in itself, stimulate reflection, there are things that the educator can do to help this process along. Kolb (1984) emphasized the importance of having opportunities to reflect on the experience:

> The active/reflective dialectic . . . is one of *transformation*, representing two opposed ways of transforming that grasp our "figurative representation" of experience—either through internal reflection, a process I will call *intention*, or active external manipulation of the external world, here called *extension*. (p. 41)

Some strategies that may foster transformative learning from experiential activities include the following:

- Setting time aside both during and after the experience for critical discourse
- Suggesting that students write about the experience in a journal or in another format
- Encouraging critical questioning—for example, suggesting that learners develop a series of questions to ask each other
- Emphasizing any discrepancies between people's perceptions of the experience and theoretical positions
- Suggesting that learners share and compare other related experiences
- Brainstorming to generate insights, thoughts, and feelings derived from the experience

- Encouraging participants to develop plans for changes in their practice or personal life
- Validating new ideas in another experience

Critical Incidents

The critical incident technique was originally designed in the 1950s as a data collection method for qualitative research (Flanagan, 1954). People are asked to describe an incident related to a specific topic or theme—a time that stands out in their memory as being especially positive or negative. A set of questions designed to elicit details of the incident are asked to determine what leads a person to interpret an experience as positive or negative.

Brookfield (1995) advocated critical incidents as a way of promoting critical reflection. The directions for a critical incident activity take the following general form:

- Think back over your last six months (or year) as a learner/teacher/worker/manager.
- Describe in about one-half page an event that was particularly positive/negative for you.
- Include when and where the incident occurred, who was involved, what was especially positive or negative about the incident, and what insights you gained from it.

The degree of structure and the number of questions addressed can vary. The ensuing discussion may be more important than completing the incident report. I usually include the following strategies:

- Modeling a critical incident and encouraging students to question it
- Suggesting learners share their critical incident in pairs with people helping each other to question the meaning of the incident
- Coaching learners to ask questions such as "Why did you say this?" or "What led you to describe it in this way?" or "What would your colleague have said at this point?"
- Moving critical questioning from the specific to the general and from content to process reflection
- Asking for some examples of incidents in the full group but definitely not requiring everyone to participate
- Including some action planning in the discussion by asking, for example, "What would you have done differently?" or "What will you do next time in such a situation?"

- Ensuring that everyone feels his or her incidents have been addressed in some way and that there are no unnoticed emotional reactions

Brookfield has gone on to develop what he calls the Critical Incident Questionnaire (CIQ) (Brookfield, 1995), a strategy for analyzing the learning process itself. The following five questions are asked:

1. At what moment in class this week were you most engaged as a learner?
2. At what moment in class this week were you most distanced as a learner?
3. What action that anyone in the room took this week did you find most affirming or helpful?
4. What action that anyone in the room took this week did you find most puzzling or confusing?
5. What surprised you the most about the class this week?

The educator makes note of themes among the responses and may include verbatim quotes to take back to the group for discussion. This modeling of critical analysis by the educator on his or her practice makes it easier for participants to engage in the same kind of analysis of their own ideas and beliefs.

Art-Based Activities

Those theorists who see transformative learning as an imaginative, intuitive process often advocate arts-based activities or the use of fiction, music, and art as stimuli for fostering transformation (Dirkx, 2001a, 2001b; Lawrence, 2012). Although we may worry about being "unacademic," especially in higher education (Shahjahan, 2004; Tisdell, 2003), the move toward being more creative and innovative as well as going outside the cognitive realm is certainly gaining momentum in adult education in general and especially among those educators whose goal it is to foster transformative learning. The proliferation of arts-based sessions at the International Transformative Learning Conferences speaks to the interest of practitioners and theorists in this approach.

In my practice, I have encouraged students to venture outside the usual boundaries and practices in which essays are the only way to express learning with remarkable outcomes. The sculpture produced by a welding instructor; the quilt sewn by a new graduate student; and the paintings, music CDs, scrapbooks, and collages I have seen over the years demonstrate clearly how arts-based learning projects not only describe transformative learning but also are transformative experiences in their creation. Following are some examples of learning projects or group activities that can be used:

- Bring in a variety of magazines, colored paper, scissors, and glue sticks and have participants create a collage that represents critical questioning of a social norm or an assumption in the field of study.
- Encourage students to write fiction or poetry as a critique of a perspective or point of view in addition to, or instead of, the traditional essay or paper.
- Give participants the option of representing the outcome of group work in a drawing rather than words.
- Encourage painting, sculpture, and music as ways of representing ideas.
- Use film, fiction, and photography to represent conflicting or alternative points of view on an issue.
- Write or put on a play as a group to demonstrate opposing ways of interpreting an event.
- Suggest a scrapbook or a series of photo collages as an alternative to a written reflective journal.

It is important for the educator to participate in learning activities proposed for students, and perhaps it is especially important with arts-based projects where people are likely to feel more self-conscious or anxious about their ability to be creative. This point was brought back to me sharply in a recent online course. I had been neglecting participating in learning activities that, online, are largely invisible to others in the group. One student asked me, "So what is your learning project?" I realized how beneficial my involvement was, and because I was experimenting with photography collages at that point, I decided to do one in relation to the course. I took great pleasure in creating the collage and even greater pleasure in posting it for students to comment on.

Individual Differences

By nature, some people are more likely to engage in critical self-reflection as a logical, analytical process than others. If we follow Mezirow's (2000) rational, cognitive model of reflection and transformation, those people who have a preference for the thinking function are most likely to follow a process that is congruent with the theory. Other individuals, though, will respond well to experiential activities (those who prefer the sensing function) or to arts-based projects (people who are more intuitive by nature). Learners who have a preference for the feeling function may engage in group and relational learning activities more readily and comfortably than they would respond to the challenges of critical questioning.

In a recent discussion in my online course on transformative learning, participants proposed that people who tend to be introverted are more likely to integrate critical reflection into their daily activities, whereas people who lead extraverted lives need to consciously make time for reflection. In a study of dialogue in the online environment, a colleague and I saw good evidence of different styles and approaches to dialogue based on psychological type preferences (Lin & Cranton, 2004).

In fostering transformative learning, the educator must maintain an awareness of individual differences, consider which events will be more likely to lead to critical self-reflection and self-knowledge in which learners, and expect variation in the processes that individuals go through. In an earlier work, I suggested strategies that may be useful for learners who have different psychological type preferences (Cranton, 2000). I summarize those points here:

- Case studies, debates, critical questioning, and analyses of theoretical perspectives are of interest to those learners who prefer the thinking function.
- Working together in pairs or groups to examine a frame of reference is helpful for individuals who prefer the feeling function.
- Concrete, experiential strategies such as field trips and simulations can assist students who prefer the sensing function to explore alternative perspectives.
- Games, metaphors, imaging, brainstorming, and arts-based activities appeal to learners who prefer the intuitive function.

Summary

Critical self-reflection and self-knowledge are fostered when individuals encounter a point of view that is different from their own. In response to this discrepancy, people can ignore the new perspective or they can be led to question the perspective they currently hold. As we go about our daily lives, we continually encounter values and assumptions that differ from our own. I think of reading, for example, letters to the editor in the local newspaper or listening to a national radio debate in Canada called *Cross Country Check Up* in which people express their opinions on issues important to our country. During these activities, I most often disregard or even feel superior to points of view that I disagree with. However, now and then, I am led to think about my own views in a critical way.

This is our job as educators—to come up with ways of creating that special moment when an individual thinks, "Oh, wait, let me reconsider this one." It can happen by chance, but we can also facilitate the process through carefully selected materials and activities. At the same time, we must keep in mind that it is *not* our job to impose points of view on others or to expect that everyone will rise to the challenges we present. It is often the case that, for a variety of reasons, people are not ready, willing, or able to make deep shifts in their habits of mind. But we still encourage reflection and hold open the possibility of transformation.

Critical questioning can be used to stimulate content, process, and premise reflection. These types of questions can lead people to make their assumptions explicit and to question the sources and consequences of their assumptions.

Consciousness-raising strategies increase self-awareness and involve looking at familiar things from a new perspective. Role plays, simulations, and life histories are useful activities for bringing things into consciousness.

Keeping a journal has a long history in adult education practice. When journals are used to encourage reflection rather than log events, they can be a powerful strategy for initiating transformative learning.

Thinking about and discussing critical incidents in participants' lives is an effective way of leading people from the specific to the general in understanding and challenging their assumptions and beliefs. A critical incident questionnaire can also be used to reflect on the process itself.

Arts-based activities provide an alternative to the traditional written word as a way of expressing beliefs and examining perspectives. As the interest in imaginative and intuitive transformation grows, practitioners are turning to creative and unusual ways to represent learners' journeys.

As in everything we do as educators, we must keep in mind that people are different. There will be no one strategy that will touch everyone, no one way that will clarify everything for every learner. Psychological type theory gives us one way of understanding these differences and selecting strategies that will be helpful to as many people as possible.

9

SUPPORTING
TRANSFORMATIVE
LEARNING

In transformative learning and emancipatory education, we recognize and work with discrepancies and unquestioned assumptions in the way we see the world. This can be a liberating and joyous process, but it can also have a dark side. We can grieve the loss of assumptions or beliefs that have long informed our lives. Family life and friendships can be disrupted. Individuals can feel isolated from their community. Daloz (2000) reminded us of the importance of a

> climate of safety in which people feel free to speak their truth, where blaming and judging are minimal, where full participation is encouraged, where a premium is placed on mutual understanding, but also where evidence and arguments may be assessed objectively and assumptions surfaced openly. (p. 114)

In discussing transformative learning for the common good, Daloz emphasized the need to seek out supportive communities.

Schapiro, Wasserman, and Gallegos (2012) described the support that comes from group work, dialogue, and relationships. They reminded us that the transformative power of dialogue comes from Rogers's (1961) work in person-centered therapy and unconditional positive regard along with Buber's (1958) notion of moving from I-it to I-thou relationships. Schapiro and colleagues (2012) proposed that transformative learning is a "direct outcome of the process of our genuine dialogue with an 'other' or others" (p. 365). It is through the support of others that we have the courage to challenge our own perspectives, assumptions, and beliefs.

The educator who fosters transformative learning has a moral responsibility to provide and arrange for support. I do not mean that we need to become counselors or make lifelong commitments to each individual we work with; however, we need to do everything we can to ensure that people are able to negotiate any difficulties they may encounter. Daloz asked what *right* we have to impose our values on our students. The stock answer to this is that we are not imposing our values but encouraging students to question their own, previously unquestioned values so that they may become more open to alternatives. But even here, we are in a sense imposing our value that it is better to become more open. Along with that imposition comes the serious obligation of making sure that people are all right.

I have worked with many students over the years whose lives have been turned upside down as a consequence, at least in part, of the kind of experiences they encountered in their studies. In Chapter 7, I described learner empowerment as a condition and an outcome of transformative learning; in Chapter 8, I discussed ways of stimulating critical self-reflection and potentially transformative learning. I now turn to the significant role of support in the process. Being supportive of learners who are engaged in transformative experiences may not look very different from being supportive in any educational context. I am not sure that this matters. We do not know when and how transformative learning will take place in any given situation, or if it will take place, yet we keep it as a goal of our practice. Throughout our work, we strive to help people feel empowered, gain self-knowledge, and explore alternative ways of thinking, and we ensure there is support to balance these challenges. To varying degrees, the theorists integrate the role of support into their understanding of transformative learning. Mezirow (2000) mentioned it briefly in relation to recognizing that the process is shared with others, whereas some, such as Belenky and Stanton (2000), placed relationships, support, and community at the center of their approach. Not everyone is comfortable becoming involved in students' lives; we each have our way of being supportive. I hope to provide enough variety in my suggestions that educators can find a way that is useful for them.

Following the thought that educators are different in the way they can be supportive, I first discuss how being authentic is central to being supportive. I then suggest strategies for building a group process that takes over some of the educators' functions. Learner networks outside of the classroom are another important source of support. Helping students understand and adapt to revised ways of thinking about themselves and the world is a part of what we must pay attention to, and in some circumstances, we can also assist people in planning a course of action based on their transformative experience. I devote sections of this chapter to each of these processes. Finally, I pay attention to conflict, ethical issues, and how people vary in their need for support.

Being Authentic

In Chapter 6, I discussed authenticity in teaching as it relates to educator roles in general, and I described research in which a colleague and I investigated authenticity. Here, drawing in part on an overview of authenticity (Cranton, 2005), I explore authenticity as it relates to supporting learners. In his now classic book, *Paradoxes of Learning: Becoming an Individual in Society,* Jarvis (1992) described people as being authentic when they choose to act so as to "foster the growth and development of each other's being" (p. 113). Jarvis saw this as an experimental and creative act where adult educators consciously have the goal of helping another person develop. Teachers and students learn together through dialogue as Freire (1970) advocated.

Freire (1970) outlined six attitudes that need to be present for meaningful and authentic dialogue:

1. Love for the world and human beings
2. Humility
3. Faith in people and their power to create and recreate
4. Trust
5. Hope that the dialogue will lead to meaning
6. Critical thinking and the continuing transformation of reality

Hollis (1998), a Jungian, helped integrate an understanding of persona (the masks we wear) with the importance of relationships in authenticity. The quality of relationships depends on how well we know ourselves and how authentically we bring ourselves to the relationship. Hollis proposed four principles of relationship:

1. What we do not know or want to accept about ourselves, we project onto others.
2. We project our wounds and longings onto others.
3. When the other person refuses responsibility for our wounds and longings, projection gives away to resentment and issues of power.
4. The only way to heal a faltering relationship is to take personal responsibility for our own individuation.

In a project where a colleague and I collected stories of transformation (Kroth & Cranton, 2014), we found that support through relationships with others fostered transformative learning. For two of the storytellers, the support of a spouse was a key element of the transformative learning process; for another the supportive community of an organization provided the context within which transformative learning could occur; and for a fourth story-teller, it was family support that allowed him to imagine a future "that is not completely damned" (p. 96).

Each of these perspectives emphasizes how authenticity is a part of relationship with others—as I have suggested elsewhere, authenticity is the expression of the genuine self in a community or with others in relationship (Cranton, 2001). Buber (1961) believed that it is only through I-thou rela-tionships with others that authenticity can be fostered. Being authentic in our relationship with students is central to being supportive. This is not to say that all teachers must have warm, deep, caring relationships with learners in order to be authentic or to be supportive. For some educators, a respectful distance is appropriate; for others, a collegial relationship works best; and for others still, a close relationship comes naturally (Cranton, 2003). What follows is a variety of suggestions for being supportive through different rela-tionship styles (with the caveat that not all educators will be comfortable with all points):

- Demonstrate interest in and concern for student learning and development.
- Share anecdotes from our own lives.
- Establish shared professional or discipline-related goals with learners.
- Illustrate and provide examples by drawing on our experience and encourage students to do the same.
- Learn from our students while they learn from us.
- Be accessible and encourage students to come to us outside of a class or session.
- Refer to where we live or our children, families, pets, or hobbies in ordinary conversation.
- Be receptive to helping students with problems and issues.
- Follow up with students, asking if they need help or are feeling comfortable.
- Be there for learners in a way that is comfortable and open.

Group Support

The educator is not the only one responsible for supporting learners in the process of transformative learning. In a cohesive learning group, people will be supportive of each other. Boyd (1989) emphasized this when he wrote that the learning group as a social system "can provide supportive structures that facilitate an individual's work in realizing personal transformation" (p. 467).

Effective, supportive groups have common identifiable characteristics:

- Commitment to the group's goals
- Conformity to and protection of group norms
- Loyalty to the group
- Acceptance of responsibility within the group
- Good communication among group members
- Willingness to be influenced by group members
- Acceptance of others' opinions
- Willingness to endure frustration on behalf of the group

The group may be seen as a learning entity (Kasl & Yorks, 2012) with the capacity to develop and transform. At the very least, the group can provide a protective and comforting blanket for those individual members who are experiencing the sad or difficult sides of transformation.

Not all groups emerge naturally into cohesive and supportive communities. Competition, conflict, power relations, and dominant voices are just a few of the many factors that can interfere with good group dynamics. How can we help students develop collaborative and supportive groups? Brookfield and Preskill (1999) listed several dispositions of democratic discussion that I see as helpful:

- *Hospitality.* An atmosphere is established in which people feel invited to participate and in which there exists a mutual receptivity to new ideas and perspectives.
- *Participation.* A community is encouraged in which everyone can be involved in significant ways.
- *Mindfulness.* An environment is set up in which people pay close attention to one another's words, listening carefully and patiently to what others say.
- *Humility.* With humility, there is the willingness to admit that our knowledge and experience are limited and incomplete and that others can teach us something.
- *Mutuality.* It is in the interest of all to care about each other's self-development.
- *Deliberation.* The classroom is one where different points of view are presented and supported by evidence, data, and logic.
- *Appreciation.* People find the space and time to express their appreciation and gratitude toward each other, raising trust and bringing people closer together.
- *Hope.* We need to maintain the hope that we can reach new understanding and work through problems, facilitated by pooling our talents.

- *Autonomy.* Individuals who are willing to take a strong stand and argue for it are important to a democratic community.

In writing about Carl Rogers's person-centered group process as transformative andragogy, O'Hara (2003) described how groups evolve to support social learning. I incorporate some of her discoveries into my guidelines for encouraging group cohesiveness and support:

- Make the process of group development open and explicit—what is done and how it is done.
- Recognize the nonrational and emotional modes of consciousness in a group.
- Look for the universal in personal stories and for connectedness to the group and the subject under consideration.
- Strive toward open rather than rule-bound systems in group processes.
- Work toward accepting ambiguity and including those with whom we disagree.
- Have faith in the wisdom of the group.
- Suggest that the group act in a social role such as writing a letter of protest or applying for increased learning resources.
- Encourage the sharing of resources and expertise within the group.
- Meet as a group outside of the usual learning environment.
- Advocate doing learning projects in small groups, writing dialogue journals, or any activities that bring people together in their learning and development.
- Ask learners to solve group problems (conflict, coping with constraints, management issues) as a group.

Learner Networks

I define a *learner network* as any sustained relationship among a group of people within a formal or informal learning context or a relationship that extends beyond the boundaries of the learning group. Within a learning group, small-group work, project teams, study partners, or peer teaching creates networks that students can rely on when they need support and guidance. Outside of the learning group, people can become members of professional associations, clubs, self-help groups, and Internet discussion groups. Going on a retreat, attending a meditation center, taking up yoga, engaging in contemplative practices, or becoming a part of any common interest activity can also provide support for an individual engaged in transformative learning, even though the activity may not be directly related to the content of the learning process. If we see transformative learning as being a deep shift in perspective, the whole of the self can be engaged; activities that foster mindfulness, peace, and quiet reflection in the presence of others can be valuable for some people.

Learner networks may form naturally, just as support within a learner group may occur without any special effort on the part of the educator. Indeed, there may not be anything about the networks unique to transformative learning. Often, for example, small subgroups that work together in a course will remain in contact throughout a program or after they have gone on to different learning experiences. Nevertheless, we should not leave this important supportive process to chance. Several strategies can be used to encourage the development of networks within a learner group:

- Using small-group activities or discussions during which learners can get to know each other and develop alliances
- Forming project groups or teams in which people work together over a longer period of time in an area of common interest
- Encouraging study partnerships or groups either informally or by setting up such groups as a part of the program
- Using peer teaching (participants sharing expertise with each other), jigsaw activities (each student or small group acquires expertise on one topic and then shares it with others), buzz groups (students join together in small groups to address specific questions), or any other techniques for bringing people together
- Creating flexibility in meeting times for groups, teams, or pairs by giving up time from the regular schedule
- Fostering liaisons by referring learners to each other when they ask questions, share concerns, or encounter problems

We should also foster participation in networks outside of the learning group whenever this is possible or appropriate. I regularly make information available to students about relevant professional associations, conferences, and electronic mailing lists. When people are engaged in a transformative process that is personal, it is important to be ready to make referrals to support groups, student services, or counseling services. Such services may be available through the institution in which we teach or, if not, through local community and social services. It is well worth making some phone calls to collect this information. We need to know when we cannot go any further in terms of providing personal support based on our knowledge of the person, the process, and our comfort level in the situation and then make the appropriate referrals. Sometimes, special interest groups are appropriate—for example, women's groups, international students' associations, or religion-based associations. It is easy and useful to help participants make contact with others who share their interests in a subject area or in personal development. I often recommend that a student contact another student with whom I have worked previously when I sense that they will be supportive for each other (with the first student's permission of course). Similarly, it can be valuable to refer learners to other educators or individuals in the community who have relevant interests or expertise. Finally, the ever-growing network of electronic mailing lists, chat rooms, and other Internet connections can provide support for some people; this resource is especially useful for anyone who does not have easy access to face-to-face groups.

In addition to referring learners as individuals or as a group to outside networks, the educator can integrate this information into a course or workshop in a variety of ways. If we refer to our own involvement in professional or personal networks, our actions act as a model for students. In some cases, it is beneficial to ask learners to share their networking experiences with the group—people may have contacts that would be of interest to others. As a part of this discussion, educators can be explicit about the important role of networks in providing support. I have also included accessing networks as a part of a learning activity in a course; for example, I have suggested that participants go to a particular electronic mailing list and bring their reactions back to the group. When learners realize how much support is available through networking, they have a lifelong resource.

Helping With Personal Adjustment

As I mentioned in the discussion of support through authenticity, educators need to make decisions about when and how they are willing to help learners with personal adjustment on an individual or situational basis. Each of us has a place where we feel comfortable and some, usually blurred, line where we begin to feel uncomfortable or out of our range of expertise. Educators regularly counsel students on job opportunities, courses or programs, thesis topics, project activities, and readings. Sometimes this advice can change a person's life. But we can be reluctant to step into what we perceive as being a student's personal life. We need to distinguish between commonly encountered difficulties students face and those difficulties where professional psychological therapy may be required. It is reasonable to support the life transitions that come through transformative experiences, but, of course, it is dangerous and unethical to step in where professional counseling is needed.

I find that providing support through personal advisement further builds my relationship with students. It demonstrates my caring and develops trust; often, students engage in deeper critical self-reflection on the basis of open, caring support. As happens in any helping relationship, self-esteem and self-confidence may be increased and anxiety allayed by open dialogue. It is difficult to provide general guidelines, but some suggestions can be made:

- Demonstrate empathy and respect for learners.
- As the relationship develops, help the student move away from dependency and into a collaborative role.
- Listen carefully.
- Provide structure when it is needed—anxious students may want structure and guidance.
- Believe in your students; have positive expectations.
- Serve as an advocate for a student in the larger system or community if needed.
- Share things about yourself.
- Act as a mirror—mirror learners' comments and answers to enhance their and your understanding.
- Avoid giving opinions or advice; encourage individuals to find their own solutions through dialogue.
- Ask questions—open-ended questions, probing questions, reflective questions, and questions for more information.

Helping learners with personal adjustment usually takes place in informal conversation. Going for a cup of tea or sitting casually at a table in the office is more conducive to this kind of interaction than is a classroom or more formal setting. Trust, respect, openness, and genuine caring for the learner are key ingredients in providing support and assistance for those who are struggling with a transformative experience.

Supporting Action

Each time I facilitate a course on transformative learning, the topic comes up of whether action on the revised habits of mind is a necessary part of transformation. Mezirow was quite clear on this. He said that action is "an integral and indispensable component of transformative learning" (1991, p. 209) and that the type of action one takes "depends on the nature of the dilemma" (1997, p. 60).

Indeed, if transformative learning involves a deep shift in perspective, as is maintained by most writers in the field, it seems it would be difficult not to act on such a change. People being different from each other, not everyone might go out and join protests or try to make changes in an organization, but I would think that some change in behavior would be evident. If we see the world differently, we respond to it differently. Even the internal act of perception makes for change. That change serves as action, and that internal action will find expression in external actions. The educator has a role in supporting actions arising out of transformative experiences.

One way of supporting actions is to help students learn to develop and implement action plans. It is one thing for a learner to say, "I now see the role of women in organizations in a completely new way," and it is something else for that learner to discuss this view with a hostile colleague, to change her behavior at work, to join a fight for pay equity, to establish a committee to investigate women's issues in her own organization, or to take a role in a national feminist group. If a person knows how to plan action based on a new perspective, such steps may not be so formidable.

Often the educator is with learners for a restricted period of time, and the action takes place after learners have left the educational setting. The skill of independently planning action can be used in any setting at any time. The very idea of action planning is a cognitive, rational one, but I try to incorporate more imaginative and relational aspects into the following action planning strategy:

- *Set a goal or create a vision.* Actions do not need to be observable to others. Some examples include making a decision to do this, writing about that in my journal, discussing this with my spouse, writing a memo to my boss on this issue, or sharing my vision with my colleagues.
- *Think about tomorrow and think about next year.* A short-term goal may be to discuss the new ideas with someone at work, but what does this mean in the long term? What will the learner do next year or five years from now that could reflect the changed perspective?
- *Consider boundaries and resources.* It may be important to bear in mind a time frame within which to work toward a goal and to consider the people who will be affected. The world cannot be changed tomorrow, and not everyone will be wildly supportive if the change is dramatic. Other considerations might include required resources, financial issues, needed expertise, or practical constraints.
- *Imagine alternatives, options, and consequences.* A part of developing critical thinking is imagining alternatives, and I think this comes into play as well in supporting action. We need to help the learner imagine and think about alternatives, options, and perhaps especially the consequences of change.

- *Consider implementation.* Sometimes having a goal is not enough—we need to think about what we will do in concrete terms to act on a change in our lives. Here the educator can help the learner by discussing ideas and offering suggestions.
- *Consider what others think.* Transformative changes in people's lives often influence others. When this occurs in the workplace, it might be helpful to encourage learners to ask others for feedback on any changes that might be visible to them. This could be done informally or in a more structured way.

Conflict and Ethical Issues

In the movie *Mona Lisa Smile* (Johanson & Newell, 2003), Katherine, the educator, challenges her students to move beyond the social norms of the 1950s that guide their lives. When her student Joan decides to marry rather than go to law school and Katherine objects, Joan challenges Katherine's right to tell her how to live. In another exchange, a conflict in values with ethical implications is clear:

Betty (student):   Don't disregard our traditions just because you're subversive.

Katherine (teacher):   Don't disrespect this class just because you're married.

Betty: Don't disrespect me just because you're not.

As educators, it is to be expected that we believe that learning is good and the more learning the better. We also believe that it is through education that individuals and groups can advance. There are strong assumptions underlying these perspectives. Does this mean that someone with limited education is inferior, unable to "advance"? Does this mean that we can or should impose our values related to the importance of education on others who do not share our point of view? Is it not possible to have a happy and peaceful life without advanced education?

At both the social and the individual levels, transformative learning is fraught with such ethical questions. When people become aware of their oppression and take action to change their situation, they are making changes in not only their own lives but also the social structure that allows the oppression to exist. This is a political and possibly an economic process which could, in some situations, lead to violence or further disadvantaging of certain groups. In the spirit of Freire, Nesbit (2004) reminded us that "education and teaching are profoundly political" (p. 17) and that attempts to advance the values of our own social class in our teaching are quite political.

At the individual level, the consequences of teaching for empowerment are no less profound. Mezirow (1991) wrote, "The educator's objective should be only that the learner learns freely and decides, on the basis of the best information available, whether or not to act and, if so, how and when" (p. 203). He went on to say that "to avoid the question of values is to opt for perpetuating the unexamined values of the status quo" (p. 203), a sentiment that Brookfield (e.g., 2005) often expressed, and one that Nesbit (2004) implied when he argued that educational systems reproduce the social relations required for capitalist production. However, the assumption underlying these points of view is that the ultimate educational achievement is to continually critically question our values and assumptions and those we see in the world around us. I believe this too but in a slightly nuanced way. Although I find it virtually impossible to argue against the educational goals of empowering the oppressed and addressing inequalities and injustices inherent in social structures, it is the idolization of the critical mind that causes me to ponder the ethical issues involved in doing so. Or perhaps it is the devaluing of concepts such as faith, conviction, and trust that is a concern. In our practitioner roles, I think we need to be diligent in asking ourselves, "What right do I have to encourage you to question what you believe? When is it a responsibility, and when is it an imposition? When is it empowering, and when is it destructive?" and "At what point do I need to leave aside my ego and thirst for learners to do as I do?"

The power relations that exist between educator and learner underline the necessity for sensitivity. A student may be influenced by an educator's values in ways that he or she would not be influenced by a peer. Usually this influence is positive; most educators are moral and good people. But even so, cultural, gender, and social differences between the educator and the student can lead to elusive ethical dilemmas and conflicts. As Smith (2004) pointed out, members of the dominant group are often unconscious and unaware of their privilege and unable to recognize their power and prejudice. Marginality is embedded in individual and institutional attitudes. Smith's example of being mistaken for a waiter at a workshop based on his being African American certainly makes this point clear. Recently, I caught myself assuming that the author of an article was female because the content included emotionality in learning. None of us is immune from these stereotypes given the culture we live in.

When making their values explicit, educators should always include alternatives and model questioning of their own values. Similarly, educators must respect the values of learners even while encouraging questioning of them. Perhaps most important, educators should reflect continually on their practice, examining the influence they have on learners and questioning the nature of that influence. Anything less fails to provide support and may be unethical.

There may be occasions when, through critical self-reflection, a student makes choices with which the educator is politically, culturally, or morally in disagreement. If everyone's interpretation is open to questioning (including the educator's), this is fine. However, if someone chooses a course of action that the educator cannot accept, he or she should withdraw, or, if the choice is potentially harmful, the educator should intervene. This very awkward and difficult situation is not one that I have personally experienced, and I imagine it occurs rarely. In most circumstances, I think the educator would be able to be open about his or her position and continue to work with the person. Supporting learners who are working toward transformative learning involves managing conflict and living with ethical issues in a responsible, professional, and open manner.

Individual Differences

Supporting transformative learning requires a good understanding of individual differences in style, psychological preferences, values, culture, race, and gender. Brookfield (2005) included two valuable chapters in his book on critical theory—one on racializing criticality and another on gendering criticality. In our efforts to support transformation, we need to be conscious of a person's preferred individual style and, as much as possible, that person's social context. Race, ethnicity, and gender are a part of personal and social being—they constitute the experience of being in the world and inform a person's worldview.

Educators can only look at the world through their own eyes. In being supportive of transformation, we need to rely on our relationship with learners and the trust, respect, and openness we build with people. The following case is based in part on a student's dialogue journal, but it is also a compilation of several experiences.

Originally from China, Chen has been in North America for several years. His psychological type preference is for extraverted sensing, but he does not have a clear secondary preference. Chen questions the cultural biases of the instrument and describes his home culture as valuing thinking to the exclusion of feeling. He suggests that this has influenced his responses to many of the items on the inventory. The educator is a Canadian White woman about the same age as the student. She has a limited knowledge of Chinese culture. Her psychological type preferences are for introverted thinking and introverted intuition. The educator and Chen met in a formal credit graduate course in adult education and then continued to work together on an independent study.

Initially, Chen wanted to accumulate as much information as possible and expressed frustration in his journal when the educator did not provide the information he was looking for. He also questioned the value of writing a journal, wrote very short entries, and said he did not know what to write about. The educator consistently expressed her belief in the value of journal writing and commented that learning was much more than the accumulation of facts. Both student and teacher were frustrated. Hostility was apparent in some of the journal entries, and humor was used to disguise some of the hostility.

There was no group of learners meeting regularly at this time, and the educator was not only trying to fix the communication problem herself but also assuming full responsibility for it. Finally, there was a turning point. The educator wrote, "I suggest that you discuss this with Ric; I know he has collected information on that topic." The next journal entries were longer, and surprisingly, Chen seemed to pay less attention to acquiring information even though this was what the educator had used to connect with him in her comment. Chen reported on his discussion with Ric. He wrote, "In my background, the teacher was always the source of all information," and later, "Ric agreed that he also expected the teacher to know everything, and he has trouble with this too." A bit later, Chen wrote, "I see it as immoral that you try to change me to be like you." The educator responded that her only intention was to encourage questioning and that she agreed it would be wrong to try to change someone. Chen took the educator's comment at face value and responded, "I'm so glad you agree with me. So, why do you question the information I give you?" This issue was not resolved.

Chen's psychological type preference should have led him to an interest in action based on his learning (which he did describe as transformative), but when asked about the practical implications of his learning or what he would now do, he ignored the questions. Eventually, he began to see how his experience would relate to his goal of teaching English as a second language, and he applied this to his thesis.

Although the educator had a good understanding of psychological type theory, she had a limited understanding of Chen's culture, and this made it hard for her to be supportive of Chen's development. Referring Chen to another student for support seemed to be the turning point in the story. When an educator works with a learner whom he or she truly cannot understand, it is important to involve others in being supportive.

Summary

Transformative learning, the process of developing more open and better justified habits of mind, frees people from constraints and is a liberating experience. But in the journey there can be times of grief, pain, conflict, and a feeling of loss of the old way of life. The educator who helps to initiate this journey is responsible for ensuring that support is available. Support comes through relationships with other people and especially through relationships with people who are authentic, open, and genuine in his or her caring. Becoming an authentic teacher is, in itself, an important developmental and transformative process for the educator, and making that explicit helps establish trust and support. Each educator needs to find his or her own best way to form relationships with learners.

Learners often turn to their peers for support, especially when they are able to identify with others who are going through a similar experience. It is not up to the educator to be everything to everyone. Establishing a good, warm, and helpful group can be critical in supporting transformative learning.

Networks that form within a group as well as those that stretch outside of the learning group are another source of support for people engaged in a transformative process. Learner networks can be based on shared personal or professional interests, and they can take the format of study groups, electronic mailing lists, or professional meetings.

Transformative experiences can lead to many changes in a person's life, some of which are difficult, personal, and hard to integrate into the fabric of being. Students may turn to the educator who set them on this path for help when things are going badly. Personal advisement is not something every educator is comfortable doing; each person needs to work within the boundaries that feel right in the particular relationship with the student and be ready to refer someone for another kind of help if that seems appropriate. I have discussed some general guidelines for helping people with personal adjustment.

Another part of supporting transformative learning is helping people act on their revised habits of mind. Often, students have already left us when they come to the point of basing actions on their learning, but we can help people prepare for that stage by planning for action with them. This is a skill that will be useful throughout a learner's life.

The very nature of transformative learning raises ethical issues. Transformation can lead to conflict in a person's life—within the family, community, and culture. Moving out from under constraints or oppressive states calls into question that which led to the oppression in the first place, and that can be anything from a person's own family through to complex social and power structures. Educators need to be conscious of the potential conflicts and the related ethical issues.

Finally, people vary in their individual styles, values, and preferences as well as in the social contexts that shape who they are. Being supportive is based on a connection with a whole person. Being aware of and sensitive to the individual and the context that has shaped that person is essential in that process.

10

THE EDUCATOR'S
TRANSFORMATIVE PROCESS

Educators who are promoting and fostering transformative learning
will benefit from understanding their personal and professional experiences with transformative learning. When we see the process from
an insider's view, we are much more likely to be able to support others; it
is meaningful to be able to say, "I have experienced the same thing; I know
what you mean."

There are far fewer studies of educator experiences with transformative
learning than there are studies of learners' experiences. Cranton and Carusetta (2004b), in their longitudinal study of how college faculty become
authentic teachers and how this is a transformative process, described how
instructors moved from concrete understandings of self, others, relationships,
context, and reflection through to multifaceted and integrative perspectives.
Similarly, in her thoughtful analysis of the role of transformative learning
in higher education, J. Moore (2005) described how she was attempting to
break free from institutional norms and barriers and in doing so she wrote,
"I am simultaneously experiencing transformations on a series of conscious
and unconscious levels" (p. 89).

Coke, Benson, and Hayes (2015) described the process of transformative learning as individuals move from being graduate students to tenure-
track professors. Mezirow's perspective on transformative learning theory
framed their study. The authors suggested that the professors "learned to
create new spaces for themselves and to redefine their roles according to new
knowledge" (p. 110). The importance of developing a mentoring framework
was stressed.

Using transformative learning theory to understand learning about
teaching, we find that in order to expand the habit of mind related to "being
an educator" we might experience the following: increasing self-awareness
through consciousness-raising activities, making our assumptions and beliefs

about our practice explicit, engaging in critical reflection on those assumptions or more intuitively imagining alternatives, engaging in dialogue with others, or developing an informed theory of practice (or a better justified perspective on practice). When we achieve new growth in our personal development, we also spontaneously achieve increased self-awareness that we bring into our professional development.

The acquisition of technical knowledge about teaching cannot be overlooked, but it would be informed by a broader-based sociolinguistic, psychological, moral, aesthetic, and philosophical base. That is, technique should not drive an educator's perspective of practice; rather, a perspective of practice should determine what technical knowledge is required. When I ventured into the exciting world of online teaching and learning, I gathered the technical skills I needed as I realized what I needed to know in order to create the kind of learning community I wanted to have.

In this chapter, I follow transformative learning theory to talk about how we can engage in a meaningful developmental journey. It is my intent to provide suggestions that each educator can consider, try on, reject, or elaborate on in order to find his or her path. If we are to foster transformative learning among our students, it is important that we experience and model the process ourselves, and what better forum than in professional development?

Awareness of Self as Educator

Most of us do not stop and think about who we are as educators. We are rushing from task to task, planning tomorrow's class, giving feedback to students, and meeting our many responsibilities in our personal and professional lives. It is easier to base our decisions about practice on what we have done before that has worked or on what we have seen or heard others do. In Chapters 6 and 9, I suggest that communications and relationships with students are founded on authenticity, bringing one's sense of self into teaching practice. This means that self-awareness is an important building block for good teaching. Self-awareness also provides the groundwork for transformative learning about teaching.

Activities such as keeping a teaching journal, setting up a teaching discussion group with colleagues, taking a workshop on reflective teaching, reading inspirational books on teaching, or completing an inventory on teaching perspectives (Pratt & Collins, 2014) are all useful ways of developing self-awareness as a teacher. Here, I suggest questions to consider for self-awareness in three domains: psychological, sociolinguistic, and epistemic (knowledge about teaching).

Psychological perspectives, as I discuss in Chapter 2, have to do with how people see themselves—their self-concepts, needs, inhibitions, anxieties, and fears. Questions we might ask ourselves include the following:

- What 10 words might I use to describe myself as an educator?
- What values do I hold in my personal life that inform my teaching?
- How would I describe my confidence or self-concept as an educator?
- How is my self-concept as an educator similar to or different from the way I think of myself outside of teaching?
- Do I feel I have personal control in my practice?
- What do I like and dislike about being an educator?
- What personal needs does being an educator fulfill?
- How does my personality suit or not suit my being an educator?
- What inhibitions or fears do I have in relation to my work?

Sociolinguistic habits of mind are based on social norms, cultural expectations, and the ways we use language. Many of the ways in which we see ourselves as educators come from the social construction of what it means to be an educator, which can be approached by considering the following questions:

- How do people in my community see educators?
- How do the media describe educators?
- Was my decision to become an educator influenced by my family, community, or culture?
- What social role should an educator have outside of his or her practice?
- How does society script or determine educator roles? How do films and television representations influence this process?
- What language is used to talk about educators' work?
- Do people treat me differently when they know I am an educator? How?
- What do my students think an educator should be like?
- What are my organization's or institution's expectations of educators?

Epistemic habits of mind are those related to knowledge and the way we acquire and use knowledge. What we know about teaching and how we learn about teaching determine, at least in part, how we see ourselves as teachers. I suggest reflection on the following questions:

- Where and how did I gain my knowledge about teaching?
- How would I describe my learning style and teaching style?
- What is the most important thing for a teacher to know?

- What is my philosophy of practice?
- How much do I know about being an educator?
- What would I like to learn about teaching?
- Am I a good teacher?
- What do others—students, colleagues, friends—say about my teaching?
- Do I always want to be a teacher?
- What is it about teaching that is most interesting?

Describing and questioning our perspectives on our practice helps to increase self-awareness and sets the stage for a more comprehensive consideration of assumptions and beliefs about being an educator.

Palmer (2004) reminded us that the path of increased self-awareness is not "onward and upward" but rather "up and down and back and around" (p. 90). Sometimes autobiographical details are too painful to be talked about openly, and Palmer suggested exploration through poetry, story, music, or art—"any metaphorical embodiment that allows us to approach the topic indirectly" (p. 90). He also emphasized asking honest, open questions of each other, those questions that invite the "soul to speak" rather than representing the views of the person asking the questions.

Revealing Assumptions

A colleague recently asked me what metaphor I would use to describe my teaching. The question drew me up short for a moment. It is the kind of question I would ask my students, but I had never really thought about it in relation to my own practice. I described a favorite photograph of mine—one of clear water running over colored rocks of various sizes—and then thought about what assumptions this metaphor might reveal. I want my practice to be clear, transparent, and fluid. My work runs through, around, over, and under the learning environment. Each individual rock (participant) is a different color, shape, and size. The water brings out the color and accentuates the differences among the rocks. Our assumptions are deeply embedded; they come from early experience, from our community and culture, and from what we know about the world. It is hard to step outside of our own points of view and isolate unarticulated and uncritically assimilated assumptions. This is as true for us as educators as it is for the people whose transformative experiences we are fostering.

Sometimes we need someone else to hold up a mirror so that we can see our assumptions. Or we need to engage in an encounter with an unusual event or a different context—one that helps us to see the assumptions we are making. We ask our students to unearth their hidden assumptions about a variety of things in sometimes quite personal arenas; we need to be able to do the same, even if we choose not to share the process with our students.

In my teaching, I include several strategies that help educators describe their transformative process. I often start the course by asking participants to tell a story about their transformative learning experience. At this point, we do not analyze the stories; they just sit there for a while as we go on to work with the theory. We come back to the stories later in the course, and we also then engage with arts-based strategies—writing poems about their stories, making collages, creating paintings, writing short (fictional) stories, or preparing playlists of favorite music. These are all optional choices, and participants are invited to propose other ways of expressing their stories. Greene (1995) passionately advocated the use of the arts as a tool for helping us to imagine the realities of worlds other than our own. Palmer (2004) wrote about using a "third thing" (a poem, a story) as a way of exploring inner issues as we project our needs onto the story. Film, artwork, fiction, poetry, and photography can be used to stimulate discussion of beliefs about teaching. Ask some questions like: How are teachers portrayed in films and fiction? What poem symbolizes something about teaching? If you were to represent the qualities of good teaching in a painting, what would you paint?

Critically Questioning and Imagining

Content, process, and premise reflection, as described in Chapter 2, provide an interesting framework for educators questioning their assumptions and beliefs about their practice. Keeping a teaching journal and discussing teaching with colleagues can form the basis for reflection. I often send my teaching journal to a trusted colleague, and he replies with comments; support; and good, critical questions about what I have written. I have sometimes shared excerpts from my teaching journal with students to obtain their reactions and insights about an issue with which I am struggling. I regularly ask learners for comments on our courses both in writing and in open discussions. All of these sources feed into my consideration of important questions:

- What did I do in that class, session, or workshop? (Content reflection)
- How did I come to do that? (Process reflection)
- Why is this important to me? (Premise reflection)

Experimentation with practice also creates a good way of questioning, reflecting, and imagining alternatives. This can be as simple as trying a new method and observing and speculating on the results or as complex as designing an action research project to systematically investigate a specific question.

Kegan (2000) beautifully illustrated the process of rejecting one's identification with uncritically assimilated assumptions by quoting Nora's speech in the closing scene of Ibsen's *A Doll's House*. As Kegan suggested, critically questioning and imagining is not simply about coming to new ideas but rather coming to "a new set of ideas about . . . ideas, about where they even come from, about who authorizes them or makes them true" (p. 57).

Consultation with professional development consultants or a human resources person can provide another perspective on our work and encourage critical reflection. Consultations take several different formats: ongoing discussion; observations of teaching; or videotaping of sessions, workshops, and readings. Even if a workshop is advertised as a how-to-do-it session, it can give us an alternative way of thinking about our practice if we approach it with that mind-set.

Essentially, any activity that encourages us to think about our teaching from a different angle or to imagine teaching in a different way is helpful, such as the following additional ideas:

- Read a book from a point of view that is different from our own (e.g., a book on presentation skills if we normally facilitate group process).
- Observe a colleague who has a different style from our own.
- Exchange teaching journals with a colleague.
- Read about research on teaching.
- Work with a "critical friend" and ask each other questions about practice.
- Create a drawing that depicts our practice and one that depicts how we do not practice.
- Read novels about teaching and learning.
- Consider what art and literature tell us about teaching and learning.

Palmer (2004) wrote about "approaching soul truth 'on the slant' through the use of third things" in a "circle of trust" with others (p. 114). Novels and drawings are "third things" that can lead us to see ourselves more clearly, especially through open, honest, and trusting dialogue with others.

Engaging Others in Dialogue

Dialogue has already come up in each of the preceding sections on self-awareness, articulating assumptions, and critical reflection, but it is important enough to elaborate on here. Educators, especially in more formal settings such as higher education, tend not to discuss their teaching with their peers. Adult educators are often working in isolation from others; much of the work is part-time, at night, or peripheral to the organization. In their integrative chapter on searching for the common ground in transformative learning theory, Wiessner and Mezirow (2000) described "talking" as one of the themes: "Once space is created for transformative learning, ways of listening and speaking within that space become important" (p. 336). Whether it is Belenky and Stanton's (2000) full-circle conversation, Kegan's (2000) "discourse of inner contractions" and "developmental discourse," Palmer's (2004) "circle of trust," or Mezirow's (2000) description of empathic listening in discourse, dialogue plays an important role. Wiessner and Mezirow also listed the use of questions and narrative as a common interest across a variety of approaches to transformative learning. We know the value of dialogue in our work with learners; we need to recognize the necessity of dialogue about teaching as a means of fostering our own development.

In order to engage in dialogue with others with a view to transformative learning about teaching, some of the following activities may be of use:

- Initiating discussion groups that meet regularly to discuss participants' practice or specific themes related to practice
- Creating a discussion group to review and question books about teaching in adult education
- Establishing a group of critical friends who meet to help participants challenge their frames of reference about teaching
- Joining one or more electronic mailing lists related to teaching (e.g., the Professional and Organizational Development Network, the Society for Teaching and Learning in Higher Education, or the Commission of Professors of Adult Education)
- Participating in conferences, such as the Adult Education Research Conference, the International Transformative Learning Conference, or the Canadian Association for Studies in Adult Education Conference

Transformation must come from within. Feeling coerced into following someone else's advice may lead to short-lived changes, but it will not result in deep and abiding shifts in perspective. Palmer (2004) followed a simple rule in his facilitation of circles of trust: "No fixing, no saving, no advising, no setting each other straight" (p. 115). He suggested that our habit of advising each other reveals its shadow side, saying something like,

> If you take my advice, you will surely solve your problem. If you take my advice but fail to solve your problem, you did not try hard enough. If you fail to take my advice, I did the best I could. So I am covered. No matter how things come out, I no longer need to worry about you or our vexing problem. (p. 117)

Our goal in engaging others in dialogue should not aim to be fixed or saved but rather to be seen and heard. Palmer said that the best service he can provide is to hold the speaker in a space where he or she can listen to the inner teacher.

Describing a Perspective on Education

Whether we call it a theory of practice, a philosophy of practice, or a perspective on education, we need to have a rationale or a mission or a vision for our teaching. What do we believe about education? What drives us to do our best? What do we hope to achieve? Even if an educator sees herself as remaining neutral, she is thereby supporting the status quo, which is, in itself, a political stance. Choosing content or strategies for facilitating a group always has an underlying meaning, whether we make it conscious or not. Naming and describing our frame of reference about education and our role within that world is a part of our transformative process.

Educators might ask:

- What is my perspective on being an educator?
- What are my goals as an educator?
- What do I do to work toward these goals, and how successful am I?

These questions can be made more concrete:

- What is my purpose in being an educator?
- How would I describe my practice in relation to this purpose?
- How do I bring myself—my beliefs, values, assumptions, and preferences—into my teaching?
- How do I see the learners I work with?
- How do I allow for change and variation in my practice?
- What methods or strategies do I usually use and why?
- What is my view of evaluation of learning, and how is this translated into practice?
- What constraints or resistances influence my practice?
- How do I know when I have done well?

My response to some of these questions might look like this:

> My purpose in being an adult educator is to facilitate individuals' learning and development, especially that which is empowering and transformative. In order to work toward this goal, I emphasize my relationship with

students. I genuinely care for the people I work with, trust them, and respect them as people and as experienced professionals. I share my expertise, support learners, and challenge them to question what they already know and what they are learning.

I am conscious of my own learning and teaching style and my values and preferences, and I try, as much as possible, to bring who I am into my relationships with students. I do not hesitate to tell anecdotes about myself and my experiences, to share my mistakes and failures, and to wonder aloud about issues that I am struggling with.

I determine the content in most of my practice in collaboration with the participants. I may introduce the area or provide an overview if it is one that is unfamiliar to participants, and I may provide guidance as to some of the things that can be included, but in general, it is the participants who choose the specific topics to work with. This approach is derived from my assumption that the students I work with are experienced and knowledgeable professionals. The methods and strategies I use in my practice are those that foster support, challenge, and collaboration. That is, I use discussion, group work, team projects, and at times individual or independent activities.

I believe that participants in my groups know better than I do what they have learned; therefore, I ask people to evaluate their own learning and, where grades are required by the institution, to assign a grade to represent that learning. I never challenge or change their evaluation. I choose not to exercise the power that is involved in the grading process.

I am fortunate in that I work primarily in graduate programs in adult education. There are very few constraints in my practice other than the constraints of scheduled meeting times (which I do not have in my online teaching) and some requirements as to deadlines for submitting grades.

I evaluate my own success based on comments from learners, people's learning projects, the nature and quality of the group processes, and the content and nature of discussions among members of the group. I also judge my success by how I feel at the end of the evening, day, or semester.

There is no one format or style for creating a perspective on education or a philosophy of practice, but this model may provide some guidance. I also enjoy philosophies that incorporate more creative components—poetry, drawings, photographs, or other illustrations.

Individuation: Teacher as Self

In Chapter 3, I describe Jung's (1971) concept of individuation as the way in which people differentiate themselves from the general, collective society. People come to see how they are both the same as and different from others, and this is a transformative process. Transformation is the emergence of the Self. (I use "Self"—as opposed to "self"—to indicate the whole of the psychological construct that represents the psyche both conscious and unconscious.)

Learning who we are as teachers—within the community of teachers and also uniquely as individuals—is a transformative journey. New educators are finding their place and learning the expectations of their profession and their institution. They are trying to fit in, and during that process, they adopt the persona of teacher, the role of teacher that society expects of them. With experience and making meaning of that experience, teachers find their own way, which is sometimes different from and sometimes the same as the teacher persona. In our research on how educators become authentic (a transformative process), my colleague and I found a clear developmental pattern (Cranton & Carusetta, 2004a). An outline of that pattern for each of the five facets of authenticity is given here:

Self-Awareness

- Fragmentation of teacher-self and Self
- Struggling to understand Self as teacher
- Integration of Self into teaching
- Understanding of Self both separate from and the same as others

Developing Awareness of Others

- Concrete, specific, unquestioned perceptions
- Consciousness of individual differences in relation to subject area acquisition
- Consciousness of others' level of personal development
- Complex, multifaceted understanding of others' diversity

Developing Relationships

- One-dimensional relationship based on rules
- Articulation of preferred nature of relationship
- A variety of ways of relating to students in different contexts
- Relationship that emphasizes the development of others' authenticity

Developing Awareness of Context

- Inflexible rules and generalizations about context
- Awareness of the influences of context on teaching and authenticity
- Critical questioning of context issues
- Setting oneself apart from context—bucking the system if necessary

Developing Critical Reflection

- Critical reflection on specific skills
- Critical reflection on teaching, institutional norms
- Content and process reflection on broader issues
- Critical questioning of premises (Why is it important to . . . ?)

At the beginning stages for each of the themes, the educator tends to follow the rules of the institution or organization, to categorize and see things in a more black-and-white fashion. As with most developmental models, people come to see the world in more complex ways, distinguish themselves from social expectations, and become able to hold seemingly contradictory points of view. Jung described the analytic process as including awareness of personal unconscious contents such as dormant character traits, attitudes, and abilities followed by discovering your role as a social being—your place in the world where you fit according to your talents and abilities, your vocation. Then in the stage of transformation, you become more fully the person you were always meant to be. Conscious development replaces unconscious behavior; meaning replaces aimlessness (Sharp, 2001). The emergence of teacher as Self is the progressive advance of consciousness.

Through the kinds of activities and strategies described in this chapter, educators can consciously move through an individuation process that takes them into a clearer and better justified frame of reference for their practice and an ever-developing idea of who they are as teachers.

Summary

I wonder if we think enough about the importance of our own learning and especially our transformative learning as practitioners. Through learning and development, we move away from a mechanistic kind of approach to selecting teaching techniques, we question our practice rather than repeating what we have done in previous sessions, and we become models for our learners.

Educators' awareness of themselves as people and practitioners is the foundation of transformative learning about teaching. In this context, I have suggested a series of questions we can ask of ourselves in each of the psychological, sociolinguistic, and epistemic frames of reference.

Articulating our assumptions about teaching can be helped by structured activities such as criteria analysis and crisis-decision simulations, or through engagement in more intuitive, arts-based strategies. Any of the processes we use to help learners become aware of their assumptions—keeping a journal, writing a life history, doing critical incidents—can be turned into a way of understanding what assumptions we might be making in our work.

Engaging in critical self-reflection and questioning regarding our practice can be done within the framework of content, process, and premise reflection. What do we do? How did we come to do it that way? Why is it important? Participation in professional development activities, engaging in action research, and discovering the influence of social norms through film and fiction can also help us to challenge our own thinking about teaching.

Dialogue is central to becoming a transformative learner about our practice. All too often, adult educators feel isolated and without support or challenge from others. I have discussed a variety of strategies for setting up the circumstances that will foster good dialogue about teaching.

When we have a rationale or a vision for our work, we are able to make meaningful choices and to think about what we do in a way that is more likely to become transformative. In this chapter, I have provided a set of questions that can be used to shape a guiding perspective on education.

Individuation is the process of distinguishing one's self from the collective of humanity and learning how we are both the same as and different from others. In the community of educators, individuation involves differentiating who we are as teachers from the teacher collective—the way teachers are expected to behave by the community, institution, and society in general. As one framework for viewing this developmental process, I have presented some results from my research on how people become authentic in their practice.

Palmer (2000) said it well:

> What a long time it can take to become the person one has always been! How often in the process we mask ourselves in faces that are not our own. How much dissolving and shaking of ego we must endure before we discover our deep identity—the true self within every human being that is the seed of authentic vocation. (p. 9)

REFERENCES

Argyris, C., & Schon, D. A. (1974). *Theory in practice: Increasing professional effectiveness.* San Francisco, CA: Jossey-Bass.

Baumgartner, L. M. (2001). An update on transformational learning. In S. Merriam (Ed.), *The new update on adult learning theory* (pp. 15–24; New Directions for Adult and Continuing Education No. 89). San Francisco, CA: Jossey-Bass.

Baumgartner, L. M. (2012). Mezirow's theory of transformative learning from 1975 to present. In E. W. Taylor & P. Cranton (Eds.), *The handbook of transformative learning: Theory, research, and practice* (pp. 99–115). San Francisco, CA: Jossey-Bass.

Belenky, M. F., Bond, L. A., & Weinstock, J. S. (1997). *A tradition that has no name.* New York, NY: Basic Books.

Belenky, M. F., Clinchy, B. M., Goldberger, N. R., & Tarule, J. M. (1986). *Women's ways of knowing: The development of self, voice, and mind.* New York, NY: Basic Books.

Belenky, M. F., & Stanton, A. (2000). Inequality, development, and connected knowing. In J. Mezirow & Associates (Eds.), *Learning as transformation: Critical perspectives on a theory in progress* (pp. 71–102). San Francisco, CA: Jossey-Bass.

Boyd, R. D. (1985). *Trust in groups: The great mother and transformative education.* Paper presented at the Annual Midwest Research-to-Practice Conference in Adult and Continuing Education, Ann Arbor, University of Michigan.

Boyd, R. D. (1989). Facilitating personal transformation in small groups. *Small Group Behavior, 20*(4), 459–474.

Boyd, R. D. (1991). *Personal transformation in small groups: A Jungian perspective.* London, UK: Routledge.

Boyd, R. D., & Myers, J. B. (1988). Transformative education. *International Journal of Lifelong Education, 7,* 261–284.

Brookfield, S. D. (1986). *Understanding and facilitating adult learning.* San Francisco, CA: Jossey-Bass.

Brookfield, S. D. (1991). *Developing critical thinkers: Challenging adults to explore alternative ways of thinking and acting.* San Francisco, CA: Jossey-Bass.

Brookfield, S. D. (1995). *Becoming a critically reflective teacher.* San Francisco, CA: Jossey-Bass.

Brookfield, S. D. (2000). Transformative learning as ideology critique. In J. Mezirow & Associates (Eds.), *Learning as transformation: Critical perspectives on a theory in progress* (pp. 131–146). San Francisco, CA: Jossey-Bass.

Brookfield, S. D. (2001). Unmasking power: Foucault and adult learning. *Canadian Journal for the Study of Adult Education, 15*(1), 1–23.

Brookfield, S. D. (2003). The praxis of transformative education: African American feminist conceptualizations. *Journal of Transformative Education, 1*(3), 212–226.

Brookfield, S. D. (2005). *The power of critical theory: Liberating adult learning and teaching.* San Francisco, CA: Jossey-Bass.

Brookfield, S. D. (2012). Critical theory and transformative learning. In E. W. Taylor & P. Cranton (Eds.), *The handbook of transformative learning: Theory, research, and practice* (pp. 131–146). San Francisco, CA: Jossey-Bass.

Brookfield, S. D., & Holst, J. D. (2010). *Radicalizing learning: Adult education for a just world.* San Francisco, CA: Jossey-Bass.

Brookfield, S. D., & Preskill, S. (1999). *Discussion as a way of teaching: Tools and techniques for democratic classrooms.* San Francisco, CA: Jossey-Bass.

Brookfield, S. D., Sheared, V., Johnson-Bailey, J., & Colin, S. (2005). Racializing the discourse of adult education. In R. J. Hill & R. Keiley (Eds.), *The 46th Annual Adult Education Research Conference* (pp. 337–344). Athens: The University of Georgia.

Buber, M. (1958). *I and thou* (R. G. Smith, Trans.). New York, NY: T&T Clark.

Buber, M. (1961). *Between man and man.* Glasgow, Scotland: Fontana Library.

Cain, C. (2013). *Quiet: The power of introverts in a world that cannot stop.* New York, NY: Broadway Paperbacks.

Campbell, V. N. (1964). Self-direction and programmed instruction for five different types of learning objectives. *Psychology in the Schools, 1*, 348–359.

Candy, P. (1991). *Self-direction for lifelong learning.* San Francisco, CA: Jossey-Bass.

Carter, T. (2000). *The voice of relationship: Transformative learning through developmental relationships in the lives of mid-career women* (Unpublished doctoral dissertation). George Washington University, Washington, DC.

Charaniya, N. K. (2012). Cultural-spiritual perspective of transformative learning. In E. W. Taylor & P. Cranton (Eds.), *The handbook of transformative learning: Theory, research, and practice* (pp. 231–244). San Francisco, CA: Jossey-Bass.

Clark, C., & Rossiter, M. (2009). Narrative learning in adulthood: Third update on adult learning theory. In S. B. Merriam (Ed.), *Third update on adult learning theory* (pp. 61–70; New Directions for Adult and Continuing Education No. 119). San Francisco, CA: Jossey-Bass.

Clark, M. C., & Wilson, A. L. (1991). Context and rationality in Mezirow's theory of transformational learning. *Adult Education Quarterly, 41*(2), 75–91.

Coady, M. M. (1939). *Masters of their own destiny.* New York, NY: Harper and Brothers.

Cohen, J. B. (2003). Hatha-yoga and transformative learning—The possibility of a union? In C. A. Wiessner, S. R. Meyer, N. Pfahl, & P. Neaman (Eds.), *Transformative learning in action: Building bridges across contexts and disciplines* (pp. 100–105; Proceedings of the Fifth International Conference on Transformative Learning, Teachers College). New York, NY: Columbia University.

Cohen, J. B. (2004). Late for school: Stories of transformation in an adult education program. *Journal of Transformative Education, 2*(2), 242–252.

Coke, P. K., Benson, S., & Hayes, M. (2015). Making meaning of experience: Navigating the transformation from graduate student to tenure-track professor. *Journal of Transformative Education, 13*(2), 110–126.

Collard, S., & Law, M. (1989). The limits of perspective transformation: A critique of Mezirow's theory. *Adult Education Quarterly, 39*, 99–107.

Cranton, P. (1994). *Understanding and promoting transformative learning.* San Francisco, CA: Jossey-Bass.

Cranton, P. (2000). Individual differences in transformative learning. In J. Mezirow & Associates (Eds.), *Learning as transformation: Critical perspectives on a theory in progress* (pp. 181–204). San Francisco, CA: Jossey-Bass.

Cranton, P. (2001). *Becoming an authentic teacher in higher education.* Malabar, FL: Kreiger.

Cranton, P. (2003). *Finding our way: A guide for adult educators.* Toronto, Ontario: Wall and Emerson.

Cranton, P. (2005). Authenticity. In L. English (Ed.), *Encyclopedia of adult education* (pp. 79–82). London, UK: Palgrave Macmillan.

Cranton, P. (2006). *Understanding and promoting transformative learning* (2nd ed.). San Francisco, CA: Jossey-Bass.

Cranton, P. (2009). From tradesperson to teacher: A transformative transition. In J. Mezirow & E. W. Taylor (Eds.), *Transformative learning in practice: Insights from community, workplace, and higher education* (pp. 182–190). San Francisco, CA: Jossey-Bass.

Cranton, P. (2011). A theory in progress. In S. B. Merriam & A. P. Grace (Eds.), *The Jossey-Bass reader on contemporary issues in adult education* (pp. 321–339). San Francisco, CA: Jossey-Bass.

Cranton, P. (2010). Transformative learning in an online environment. *International Journal of Adult Vocational Education and Technology, 1*(2), 1–9.

Cranton, P. (2012). *Planning instruction for adult learners* (3rd ed.). Toronto, Ontario: Wall & Emerson.

Cranton, P. (2014). Distributing power through curriculum development. In V. C. X. Wang & V. Byrant (Eds.), *Andragogical and pedagogical methods for curriculum and program development* (pp. 22–34). Hershey, PA: IGI Global.

Cranton, P., & Carusetta, E. (2004a). Developing authenticity as a transformative process. *Journal of Transformative Education, 2*(4), 276–293.

Cranton, P., & Carusetta, E. (2004b). Perspectives on authenticity in teaching. *Adult Education Quarterly, 55*(1), 5–22.

Cranton, P., & Dirkx, J. (2005). *Integrating theoretical perspectives through online dialogue.* Paper presented at the 6th International Transformative Learning Conference, East Lansing, MI.

Cranton, P., & Knoop, R. (1995). Assessing psychological type: The PET type check. *General, Social, and Genetic Psychological Monographs, 121*(2), 247–274. Also available at www.learningstyles.ca

Cranton, P., & Roy, M. (2003). When the bottom falls out of the bucket: Toward a holistic perspective on transformative learning. *Journal of Transformative Education, 1*(2), 86–98.

Cranton, P., & Taylor, E. W. (2012). Transformative learning: Seeking a more unified theory. In E. W. Taylor & P. Cranton (Eds.), *The handbook of transformative learning: Theory, research, and practice* (pp. 1–20). San Francisco, CA: Jossey-Bass.

Cunningham, P. (1992). From Freire to feminism: The North American experience with critical pedagogy. *Adult Education Quarterly, 42*(3), 180–191.

Daloz, L. (1988). The story of Gladys who refused to grow. *Lifelong Learning, 2,* 47.

Daloz, L. (1999). *Mentor: Guiding the journey of adult learners.* San Francisco, CA: Jossey-Bass.

Daloz, L. (2000). Transformative learning for the common good. In J. Mezirow & Associates (Eds.), *Learning as transformation: Critical perspectives on a theory in progress* (pp. 103–124). San Francisco, CA: Jossey-Bass.

Dewey, J. (1933). *How we think.* New York, NY: Heath.

Dewey, J. (1938). *Experience and education.* New York, NY: Collier Books.

Dirkx, J. (1997). Nurturing soul in adult education. In P. Cranton (Ed.), *Transformative learning in action: Insights from practice* (pp. 79–88; New Directions for Adult and Continuing Education No. 74). San Francisco, CA: Jossey-Bass.

Dirkx, J. (1998). Transformative learning theory in the practice of adult education: An overview. *PAACE Journal of Lifelong Learning, 7,* 1–14.

Dirkx, J. (2000). After the burning bush: Transformative learning as imaginative engagement with everyday experience. In C. A. Wiessner, S. Meyer, & D. Fuller (Eds.), *Challenges of practice: Transformative learning in action* (pp. 247–252; Proceedings of the Third International Conference on Transformative Learning, Teachers College). New York, NY: Columbia University.

Dirkx, J. (2001a). Images, transformative learning and the work of soul. *Adult Learning, 12*(3), 15–16.

Dirkx, J. (2001b). The power of feelings: Emotion, imagination, and the construction of meaning in adult learning. In S. Merriam (Ed.), *The new update on adult learning theory* (pp. 63–72; New Directions for Adult and Continuing Education No. 89). San Francisco, CA: Jossey-Bass.

Dirkx, J. (2012). Nurturing soul work: A Jungian approach to transformative learning. In E. W. Taylor & P. Cranton (Eds.), *The handbook of transformative learning: Theory, research, and practice* (pp. 116–130). San Francisco, CA: Jossey-Bass.

Dirkx, J. M., Mezirow, J., & Cranton, P. (2006). Musings and reflections on the meaning, context, and process of transformative learning: A dialogue between John M. Dirkx and Jack Mezirow. *Journal of Transformative Education, 4*(2), 123–139.

Dominicé, P. (2000). *Learning from our lives: Using educational biographies with adults.* San Francisco, CA: Jossey-Bass.

Ebert, O., Burford, M. L., & Brian, D. (2003). Highlander: Education for change. *Journal of Transformative Education, 1*(4), 321–340.

English, L. M. (2004). *Feminine/feminist: A poststructural reading of relational learning in women's social action organizations.* Proceedings of the joint Adult Education Research Conference and Canadian Association for the Study of Adult Education 23rd National Conference, May 28–30, 2004, University of Victoria, Victoria, British Columbia. Retrieved from http://www.oise.utoronto.ca/CASAE/cnf2004/2004onlineProceedings/E_G.pdf

English, L. M., & Irving, C. U. (2012). Women and transformative learning. In E. W. Taylor & P. Cranton (Eds.), *The handbook of transformative learning: Theory, research, and practice* (pp. 245–259). San Francisco, CA: Jossey-Bass.

Feller, A., Jensen, A., Marie, D., Peddigrew, B., Clinchard-Sepeda, L., & Campbell, E. (2004). Quadrinity online: Toward a fuller expression of transformative learning. *Journal of Transformative Education, 2*(3), 219–230.

Fenwick, T. (1998). Questioning the concept of the learning organization. In S. M. Scott, B. Spencer, & A. M. Thomas (Eds.), *Learning for life: Canadian readings in adult education.* Toronto, Ontario: Thompson.

Flanagan, J. (1954). The critical incident technique. *Psychological Bulletin, 51,* 132–136.

Foucault, M. (1980). *Power/knowledge: Selected interviews and other writings, 1972–1977.* New York, NY: Pantheon.

Frankl, V. (1984). *Man's search for meaning.* New York, NY: Touchstone.

Freire, P. (1970). *Pedagogy of the oppressed.* New York, NY: Herder and Herder.

Freud, S. (1963). Civilization and its Discontents. London: Hogarth Press.

Gardner, H., Kornhaber, M. L., & Wake, W. K. (1996). *Intelligence: Multiple perspectives.* New York, NY: Harcourt Brace.

Gilly, M. S. (2004). Experiencing transformative education in the "corridors" of a non-traditional doctoral program. *Journal of Transformative Education, 2*(3), 231–242.

Goleman, D. (1998). *Working with emotional intelligence.* New York, NY: Bantam Books.

Goleman, D. (2011). *The brain and emotional intelligence: New insights.* Northampton, MA: More Than Sound.

Gozawa, J. (2003). Transforming learning as disorienting dilemma. In C. A. Wiessner, S. R. Meyer, N. Pfhal, & P. Neaman (Eds.), *Transformative learning in action: Building bridges across contexts and disciplines* (pp. 202–207; Proceedings of the Fifth International Conference on Transformative Learning, Teachers College). New York, NY: Columbia University.

Greene, M. (1995). *Releasing the imagination: Essays on education, the arts, and social change.* San Francisco, CA: Jossey-Bass.

Gunnlaugson, O. (2003). Toward an integral education for the ecozoic era: A case study in transforming the global learning community of Holma College of Integral Studies. *Journal of Transformative Education, 2*(4), 313–335.

Habermas, J. (1971). *Knowledge and human interests.* Boston, MA: Beacon Press.

Habermas, J. (1984). *The theory of communicative action.* Boston, MA: Beacon Press.

Harrison, J. (1961). *Learning and living 1790–1960.* London, UK: Routledge and Kegan Paul.

Hart, M. (1990). Critical theory and beyond: Further perspectives on emancipatory education. *Adult Education Quarterly, 40,* 125–138.

Hayes, E., & Flannery, D. (2000). *Women as learners: The significance of gender in adult learning.* San Francisco, CA: Jossey-Bass.

Herman, L. (2003). Engaging the disturbing images of evil. In C. A. Wiessner, S. R. Meyer, N. Pfhal, & P. Neaman (Eds.), *Transformative learning in action: Building bridges across contexts and disciplines* (pp. 246–248; Proceedings of the Fifth International Conference on Transformative Learning, Teachers College). New York, NY: Columbia University.

Hillman, J. (2000). Peaks and vales. In B. Sells (Ed.), *Working with images.* Woodstock, CT: Spring Publishers.

Hollis, J. (1998). *Eden project: In search of the magical other.* Toronto, Ontario: Inner City Books.

Hollis, J. (2001). *Creating a life: Finding your individual path.* Toronto, Ontario: Inner City Books.

Jarvis, P. (1992). *Paradoxes of learning: Becoming an individual in society.* San Francisco, CA: Jossey-Bass.

Johanson, F. (Producer), & Newell, M. (Director). (2003). *Mona Lisa smile* [motion picture]. United States: Columbia Pictures.

Johnson, R. (2003). Autobiography and transformative learning: Narrative in search of self. *Journal of Transformative Education, 1*(3), 227–245.

Jung, C. (1968). *Analytical psychology: Its theory and practice.* New York: Random House.

Jung, C. (1971). *Psychological types.* Princeton, NJ: Princeton University Press. (Original work published 1921)

Kasl, E., & Elias, D. (2000). Creating new habits of mind in small groups. In J. Mezirow & Associates (Eds.), *Learning as transformation: Critical perspectives on a theory in progress* (pp. 229–252). San Francisco, CA: Jossey-Bass.

Kasl, E., Marsick, V. J., & Dechant, K. (1997). Teams as learners: A research-based model of team learning. *Journal of Applied Behavioral Science, 33*, 227–246.

Kasl, E., & Yorks, L. (2012). Learning to be what we know: The pivotal role of presentational knowing in transformative learning. In E. W. Taylor & P. Cranton (Eds.), *The handbook of transformative learning: Theory, research, and practice* (pp. 503–519). San Francisco, CA: Jossey-Bass.

Kegan, R. (1994). *In over our heads.* Cambridge, MA: Harvard University Press.

Kegan, R. (2000). What "form" transforms? A constructive-developmental approach to transformative learning. In J. Mezirow & Associates (Eds.), *Learning as transformation: Critical perspectives on a theory in progress* (pp. 35–70). San Francisco, CA: Jossey-Bass.

King, P., & Kitchener, K. (1994). *Developing reflective judgment.* San Francisco, CA: Jossey-Bass.

Knowles, M. (1975). *Self-directed learning: A guide for learners and teachers.* Chicago, IL: Follett.

Knowles, M. (1980). *The modern practice of adult education: From pedagogy to andragogy.* New York, NY: Cambridge.

Kolb, D. (1984). *Experiential learning: Experience as the source of learning and development.* Englewood Cliffs, NJ: Prentice Hall.

Kolb, D. (1999). *Learning style inventory.* Boston, MA: Hay/McBer.

Kolb, D. (2015). *Experiential learning: Experience as the source of learning and development* (2nd ed.). Englewood Cliffs, NJ: Prentice Hall.

Kreber, C. (2012). Critical reflection and transformative learning. In E. W. Taylor & P. Cranton (Eds.), *The handbook of transformative learning: Theory, research, and practice* (pp. 323–341). San Francisco, CA: Jossey-Bass.

Kroth, M., & Cranton, P. (2014). *Stories of transformative learning*. Rotterdam, the Netherlands: Sense.

Kucukaydin, I. (2010). Counter-learning under oppression. *Adult Education Quarterly, 60*(3), 215–232.

Kucukaydin, I., & Cranton, P. (2012). Participatory learning in formal adult education contexts. *International Journal of Adult Vocational Education and Technology, 3*(1), 1–13.

Lawrence, R. (2012). Transformative learning through artistic expression: Getting out of our heads. In E. W. Taylor & P. Cranton (Eds.), *The handbook of transformative learning: Theory, research, and practice* (pp. 471–485). San Francisco, CA: Jossey-Bass.

Lennard, D., Thompson, T., & Booth, G. (2003). The artist's inquiry: Fostering transformative learning through the arts. In C. A. Wiessner, S. R. Meyer, N. Pfhal, & P. Neaman (Eds.), *Transformative learning in action: Building bridges across contexts and disciplines* (pp. 269–273; Proceedings of the Fifth International Conference on Transformative Learning, Teachers College). New York, NY: Columbia University.

Lin, L., & Cranton, P. (2004). Dancing to different drummers: Individual differences and online learning. *Creative College Teaching Journal, 1*(1), 30–40.

Lindeman, E. C. (1926). *The meaning of adult education*. New York, NY: New Republic.

MacKeracher, D. (2004). *Making sense of adult learning* (2nd ed.). Toronto, Ontario: University of Toronto Press.

MacKeracher, D. (2009). Social change in historical perspective. In P. Cranton & L. M. English (Eds.), *Reaching out across the border: Canadian perspectives in adult education* (pp. 25–36; New Directions for Adult and Continuing Education No. 124). San Francisco, CA: Jossey-Bass.

MacKeracher, D. (2012). The role of experience in transformative learning. In E. W. Taylor & P. Cranton (Eds.), *The handbook of transformative learning: Theory, research, and practice* (pp. 342–354). San Francisco, CA: Jossey-Bass.

Marcuse, H. (1978). *The aesthetic dimension: Toward a critique of Marxist aesthetics*. Boston, MA: Beacon Press.

Markos, L., & McWhinney, W. (2004). Editors' perspectives: Building on and toward a shared vision. *Journal of Transformative Education, 2*(2), 75–79.

Mejiuni, O. (2012). *Women and power: Education, religion and identity*. Ibadan, Nigeria: University Press.

Merriam, S. (2004). The role of cognitive development in Mezirow's transformative learning theory. *Adult Education Quarterly, 55*(1), 60–68.

Merriam, S., & Brockett, R. (1997). *The profession and practice of adult education: An introduction*. San Francisco, CA: Jossey-Bass.

Mezirow, J. (1975). *Education for perspective transformation: Women's reentry programs in community colleges*. New York, NY: Center for Adult Education, Teachers College, Columbia University.

Mezirow, J. (1978). Perspective transformation. *Adult Education, 28*, 100–110.

Mezirow, J. (1981). A critical theory of adult learning and education. *Adult Education, 32,* 3–24.

Mezirow, J. (1985). A critical theory of self-directed learning. In S. Brookfield (Ed.), *Self-directed learning: From theory to practice* (pp. 17–30; New Directions for Continuing Education No. 25). San Francisco, CA: Jossey-Bass.

Mezirow, J. (1989). Transformative learning and social action: A response to Collard and Law. *Adult Education Quarterly, 39,* 169–175.

Mezirow, J. (Ed.). (1990). *Fostering critical reflection in adulthood: A guide to transformative and emancipatory learning.* San Francisco, CA: Jossey-Bass.

Mezirow, J. (1991). *Transformative dimensions of adult learning.* San Francisco, CA: Jossey-Bass.

Mezirow, J. (1997). Transformative theory out of context. *Adult Education Quarterly, 48*(1), 60–62.

Mezirow, J. (2000). Learning to think like an adult. In J. Mezirow & Associates (Eds.), *Learning as transformation: Critical perspectives on a theory in progress* (pp. 3–33). San Francisco, CA: Jossey-Bass.

Mezirow, J. (2003a). Epistemology of transformative learning. In C. Wiessner, S. Meyer, N. Pfhal, & P. Neaman (Eds.), *Transformative learning in action: Building bridges across contexts and disciplines* (pp. 310–314; Proceedings of the Fifth International Conference on Transformative Learning, Teachers College). New York, NY: Columbia University.

Mezirow, J. (2003b). Transformative learning as discourse. *Journal of Transformative Education, 1*(1), 58–63.

Mezirow, J. (2004). Forum content on Sharan Merriam's "The role of cognitive development in Mezirow's transformational learning theory." *Adult Education Quarterly, 55*(1), 69–70.

Mezirow, J. (2012). Learning to think like an adult: Core concepts of transformation theory. In E. W. Taylor & P. Cranton (Eds.), *The handbook of transformative learning: Theory, research, and practice* (pp. 73–96). San Francisco, CA: Jossey-Bass.

Moore, J. (2005). Is higher education ready for transformative learning? A question explored in the study of sustainability. *Journal of Transformative Education, 3*(1), 76–91.

Moore, T. (1996). *The re-enchantment of everyday life.* New York, NY: HarperCollins.

Myers, I. B. (1980). *Gifts differing.* Palo Alto, CA: Consulting Psychologists Press.

Nesbit, T. (2004). Class and teaching. In R. St. Clair & J. A. Sandlin (Eds.), *Promoting critical practice in adult education* (pp. 15–24; New Directions for Adult and Continuing Education No. 102). San Francisco, CA: Jossey-Bass.

Nesbit, T., Brigham, S. M., Taber, N., & Gibb, T. (2013). *Building on critical traditions: Adult education and learning in Canada.* Toronto, Ontario: Thompson.

Newman, M. (2012). Calling transformative learning into question: Some mutinous thoughts. *Adult Education Quarterly, 62*(1), 36–55.

O'Hara, M. (2003). Cultivating consciousness: Carl R. Rogers' person-centered group process as transformative andragogy. *Journal of Transformative Education, 1*(1), 64–79.

Ontario Institute for Studies in Education. (2004, November). *The Transformative Learning Centre.* Retrieved from http://legacy.oise.utoronto.ca/research/tlcentre/about.html

O'Sullivan, E. (2003). The ecological terrain of transformative learning: A vision statement. In C. A. Wiessner, S. R. Meyer, N. Pfhal, & P. Neaman (Eds.), *Transformative learning in action: Building bridges across contexts and disciplines* (pp. 352–357; Proceedings of the Fifth International Conference on Transformative Learning, Teachers College). New York, NY: Columbia University.

O'Sullivan, E. (2012). Deep transformation: Forging a planetary world view. In E. W. Taylor & P. Cranton (Eds.), *The handbook of transformative learning: Theory, research, and practice* (pp. 162–177). San Francisco, CA: Jossey-Bass.

Palmer, P. (1998). *The courage to teach: Exploring the inner landscape of a teacher's life.* San Francisco, CA: Jossey-Bass.

Palmer, P. (2000). *Let your life speak: Listening for the voice of vocation.* San Francisco, CA: Jossey-Bass.

Palmer, P. (2004). *A hidden wholeness: The journey toward an undivided life.* San Francisco, CA: Jossey-Bass.

Perry, W. G. (1970). *Forms of intellectual and ethical development in the college years.* Austin, TX: Holt, Rinehart, & Winston.

Pratt, D. D., & Collins, J. B. (2014). Teaching Perspectives Inventory [Online measurement instrument]. Retrieved from http://www.teachingperspectives.com/

Progoff, I. (1992). *At a journal workshop: Writing to ace the power of the unconscious and evoke creative ability.* New York, NY: Penguin Putnam.

Quindlen, A. (2002). *Blessings.* New York, NY: Random House.

Robinson, P. (2004). Meditation: Its role in transformative learning and the fostering of an integrative vision for higher education. *Journal of Transformative Education, 2*(2), 107–122.

Rogers, C. R. (1961). *On becoming a person: A therapist's view of psychotherapy.* Boston, MA: Houghton-Mifflin.

Sawyer, L. (2003). Transformative learning at the intersection of body, mind, and spirit. In C. A. Wiessner, S. R. Meyer, N. Pfhal, & P. Neaman (Eds.), *Transformative learning in action: Building bridges across contexts and disciplines* (pp. 369–374; Proceedings of the Fifth International Conference on Transformative Learning, Teachers College). New York, NY: Columbia University.

Schapiro, S. A., Wasserman, I. L., & Gallegos, P. V. (2012). Group work and dialogue: Spaces and processes for transformative learning in relationships. In E. W. Taylor & P. Cranton (Eds.), *The handbook of transformative learning: Theory, research, and practice* (pp. 355–372). San Francisco, CA: Jossey-Bass.

Scott, S. (2003). The social construction of transformation. *Journal of Transformative Education, 1*(3), 264–284.

Senge, P. M. (1990). *The fifth discipline: The art and practice of the learning organization.* New York, NY: Doubleday.

Shahjahan, R. A. (2004). Centering spirituality in the academy: Toward a transformative way of teaching and learning. *Journal of Transformative Education, 2*(4), 294–312.

Sharp, D. (1987). *Personality types: Jung's model of typology.* Toronto, Ontario: Inner City Books.

Sharp, D. (2001). *Digesting Jung: Food for the journey.* Toronto, Ontario: Inner City Books.

Smith, S. (2004). Insider and outsider status: An African American perspective. In M. Wise & M. Glowacki-Dudka (Eds.), *Embracing and enhancing the margins of adult education* (pp. 57–65; New Directions for Adult and Continuing Education No. 104). San Francisco, CA: Jossey-Bass.

Stuckey, H., Taylor, E. W., & Cranton, P. (2014). Assessing transformative learning processes and outcomes. *Journal of Transformative Education, 11*(4), 211–228.

Taylor, E. W. (2000). Analyzing research on transformative learning theory. In J. Mezirow & Associates (Eds.), *Learning as transformation: Critical perspectives on a theory in progress* (pp. 285–328). San Francisco, CA: Jossey-Bass.

Taylor, E. W. (2008). Transformative learning theory. In S. B. Merriam (Ed.), *Third update on adult learning theory* (pp. 5–16; New Directions for Adult and Continuing Education No. 119). San Francisco, CA: Jossey-Bass.

Taylor, E. W. (2009). Fostering transformative learning. In J. Mezirow & E. W. Taylor (Eds.), *Transformative learning in practice: Insights from community, workplace, and higher education* (pp. 3–17). San Francisco, CA: Jossey-Bass.

Taylor, E. W., & Snyder, M. (2012). A critical review of research on transformative learning theory, 2006–2010. In E. W. Taylor & P. Cranton (Eds.), *The handbook of transformative learning: Theory, research, and practice* (pp. 37–55). San Francisco, CA: Jossey-Bass.

Taylor, K. (2000). Teaching with developmental intention. In J. Mezirow & Associates (Eds.), *Learning as transformation: Critical perspective on a theory in progress* (pp. 151–180). San Francisco, CA: Jossey-Bass.

Taylor, K., & Elias, D. (2012). Transformative learning: A developmental perspective. In E. W. Taylor & P. Cranton (Eds.), *The handbook of transformative learning: Theory, research, and practice* (pp. 147–161). San Francisco, CA: Jossey-Bass.

Tennant, M. (1993). Perspective transformation and adult development. *Adult Education Quarterly, 44*(1), 34–42.

Tennant, M. (2012). *The learning self: Understanding the potential for transformation.* San Francisco, CA: Jossey-Bass.

Tisdell, E. J. (2003). *Exploring spirituality and culture in adult and higher education.* San Francisco, CA: Jossey-Bass.

Tisdell, E. J., & Tolliver, D. E. (2001). The role of spirituality in culturally relevant and transformative adult education. *Adult Learning, 12*(3), 13–14.

Torres, C. A. (2003). Paulo Freire, education and transformative social justice learning. In C. A. Wiessner, S. R. Meyer, N. Pfhal, & P. Neaman (Eds.), *Transformative learning in action: Building bridges across contexts and disciplines* (pp. 427–430; Proceedings of the Fifth International Conference on Transformative Learning, Teachers College). New York, NY: Columbia University.

Tyler, J. A., & Swartz, A. L. (2012). Storytelling and transformative learning. In E. W. Taylor & P. Cranton (Eds.), *The handbook of transformative learning: Theory, research, and practice* (pp. 455–470). San Francisco, CA: Jossey-Bass.

Vella, J. (2002). *Learning to listen, learning to teach: The power of dialogue in educating adults.* San Francisco, CA: Jossey-Bass.

Watkins, K., & Marsick, V. J. (1993). *Sculpting the learning organization: Lessons in the art and science of systemic change.* San Francisco, CA: Jossey-Bass.

Watkins, K. E., Marsick, V. J., & Faller, P. G. (2012). Transformative learning in the workplace: Leading learning for self and organizational change. In E. W. Taylor & P. Cranton (Eds.), *The handbook of transformative learning: Theory, research, and practice* (pp. 373–387). San Francisco, CA: Jossey-Bass.

Watkins, M. (2000). *Invisible guests: The development of imaginal dialogue.* Woodstock, CT: Spring Publishers.

Wiessner, C. A. (2000). Passin' it on. In C. A. Wiessner, S. Meyer, & D. Fuller (Eds.), *Challenges of practice: Transformative learning in action* (pp. 147–152; Proceedings of the Third International Conference on Transformative Learning, Teachers College). New York, NY: Columbia University.

Wiessner, C. A., & Mezirow, J. (2000). Theory building and the search for common ground. In J. Mezirow & Associates (Eds.), *Learning as transformation: Critical perspectives on a theory in progress* (pp. 329–358). San Francisco, CA: Jossey-Bass.

Wright, B., Cranton, P., & Quigley, A. (2007). *Literacy educators' perspectives of transformation and authenticity.* Paper presented at the 48th Annual Adult Education Research Conference, Halifax, Nova Scotia.

Yorks, L., & Marsick, V. J. (2000). Organizational learning and transformation. In J. Mezirow & Associates (Eds.), *Learning as transformation: Critical perspectives on a theory in progress* (pp. 253–281). San Francisco, CA: Jossey-Bass.

Yukl, G. (1989). *Leadership in organizations* (2nd ed.). Upper Saddle River, NJ: Prentice-Hall.

ABOUT THE AUTHOR

Patricia Cranton received her BEd with distinction (1971) and her MSc (1973) from the University of Calgary and her PhD (1976) from the University of Toronto. Among the awards she has received are the Ontario Distinguished Scholarship award, the Ontario Confederation of University Faculty Association's Teaching Award, and the Lieutenant Governor's Laurel Award. In 2014, she was inducted into the International Adult Continuing Education Hall of Fame. In 2016, she received the Order of Canada for her contributions to higher and adult education.

Patricia is a retired professor of adult and higher education who is currently affiliated with the University of New Brunswick in Canada and Teachers College, Columbia University, in the United States. She has held positions at McGill University, Brock University, University of New Brunswick, St. Francis Xavier University, and Pennsylvania State University and has been teaching courses in transformative learning for 20 years.

Cranton has written or edited several books, most recently *Planning Instruction for Adult Learners* (Wall & Emerson, 2012), *The Handbook of Transformative Learning: Theory, Research and Practice* (Jossey-Bass, 2012), *Stories of Transformative Learning* (Sense Publishers, 2014), *A Guide to Research for Educators and Trainers of Adults* (Krieger Publishers, 2015), *A Novel Idea: Researching Transformative Learning in Fiction* (Sense Publishers, 2015), and *Measuring and Analyzing Informal Learning in the Digital Age* (IGI Publishers, 2015).

models for, 47
process reflection questions for, 109
psychological type theory and, 75
revision of habits of mind and, 75
"Tammy" and "Martin" examples of,
    105–7
critical theory, 35–36
    tasks for, 99–100
critical thinking, 79–80, 83

Daloz, L., 122
"David" empowerment example, 47–48
debriefing, 111–12
democratic discussion, dispositions of,
    126–27
democratic participation, 36
development, dimensions of, 58
developmental perspective, 58, 60
developmental relationships, 33
developmental transformation, 59
    five dimensions of, 58
Dewey, J.
    Experience and Education by, 115
    on rational problem solving, 116
    reflection defined by, 25–26
differentiation
    Jungian psychology on, 72
    psychological type theory and, 71
Dirkx, J., 39–40
    soul work and, 53
disciplinary power, 84–86, 96–97,
    98, 99
    journals as manifestation of, 114
discourse and dialogue
    activities for fostering, 144
    authors on importance of, 144
    critical self-reflection in, 97
    definition of, 19, 51
    empowerment through, 97–98
    extrarational perspective and, 52
    learners stories on, 52
    Mezirow on, 9, 74–75
    Palmer on circles of trust in, 144–45
    psychological type theory and, 74–75
    reflective judgment in, 97

role of, 51–52
strategies for equal participation
    in, 98
transformative learning theory
    and, 19
discussion circle, 86, 94, 102, 103
disorienting event, 73–74
    critical reflection and, 48–50
    psychological type and, 73–74
    "Sheila" example, 48–49
distorted meaning perspectives, 22, 105
divergent thinking, 100
A Doll's House (Ibsen), 143
dualistic thinking, 32

ecological view
    "integrally informed" education
        and, 39
    O'Sullivan on, 38–39
educational biographies, 112–13
educator roles, 78, 90
    in art-based activities, 119
    authenticity in, 87–89
    communicative knowledge in,
        81–82
    emancipatory learning and,
        82–83, 87
    perspective transformation in, 82
    power in, 84–87
    technical knowledge and, 79–81
educators transformative process, 149
    activities for, 139
    crisis-decision simulations in, 148
    criteria analysis in, 148
    critically questioning and imagining,
        142–43
    describing a perspective on
        education, 145–46
    engaging others in dialogue, 143–45
    experience studies on, 138
    individuation of teacher as Self,
        146–48
    Palmer on, 141
    revealing assumptions in, 141–42
    self-awareness in, 139–41

encouraging group cohesiveness and
support, 127
for helping with personal
adjustment, 130
for journal writing, 115

Habermas, J.
Mezirow using work of, 17
system world described by, 24
three kinds of knowledge by,
9–11, 17
habits of mind
aesthetic, 21–22
content reflection questions and, 108
distorted assumptions of, 22, 25
epistemic, 19–20, 140–41
frames of reference and, 29
as inter-related, 22
Mezirow on, 29
moral-ethical, 21
philosophical, 21, 29
psychological, 20–21
questioning and, 107–10
reflective questions for, 25–26, 28
revisions of, 75–76
sociolinguistic, 20, 82, 140
stage theories of development, 23
types of, 19–22
unquestioned, 22–25
*The Handbook of Transformative
Learning: Theory, Research
and Practice* (Cranton and
Taylor), 41
Highlander Research and Education
Center, 34–35
Highland Folk School. *See* Highlander
Research and Education Center
holistic theory, transformative
learning, 41
Hollis, J., 124
Holma College of Integral Studies, 39
Horton, M., 34–35
humanism, ix, 4, 8, 104
humanity, 8, 24, 71–72, 149

Ibsen, H., *A Doll's House* by, 143
ideology critique, ix, 36, 83
definition of, 109
imaginative perception, 110
incremental transformation, 19, 55–56
learner experience with, 57–58
individual differences. *See also*
psychological functions;
psychological type theory
Brookfield on, 134
critical self-reflection and, 119–20
educator sensitivity to various, 134
empowerment and, 102–3
supporting transformative learning
with, 134–35
worldview informed by, 134
individuation
Jungian psychology and, 31, 40–41,
72–73, 146
psychological type theory and, 72, 73
teacher as Self, 147–48
instrumental learning, 12
educator roles and, 79
Mezirow defining, 9–10
integrative thinking, 32
International Transformative Learning
Conference, ix, 17, 30, 118, 144
introversion
description of, 63–64
functions of, 69–70
types of, 67–70
intuitive functions, 65, 66, 71, 120

"Jim" extrarational approach example,
54–55
Journal of Transformative Education, ix,
40, 42
journals
critical reflection and, 113–15
disciplinary power and, 114
Progoff on use of, 114
suggestions for writing, 114
Jung, C.
on consciousness, 110

Palmer, P.
  on authentic vocation, 149
  on circles of trust, 144–45
  on educators transformative
    process, 141
  "third things" in critical questioning
    by, 143
pedagogy, x, 4
perceptive (or irrational) functions,
    65, 71
personal adjustment, helping
    learners with
  boundaries in, 129–30
  suggestions for, 130
Personal Empowerment through Type
    (PET), 70, 103
personal transformation, 39
perspective on education
  example of, 145–46
  questions for educators in, 145
perspective transformation, ix, 75
  definition of, 16–17
  in educator roles, 82
  process of, 16
PET. *See* Personal Empowerment
    through Type
philosophical habits of mind, 21, 29
power
  asymmetrical relationships,
    17–18
  conflict and ethical issues
    regarding, 133
  disciplinary, 84–86, 96–97, 98,
    99, 114
  personal and position concepts of,
    84, 86
  relationships and, 93–95
  responsibly exercising, 95–97
  sovereign, 86, 95, 96
  surveillance, 85, 87
power states, 104
practical knowledge, 10
premise reflection, 26–27
  in educators transformative
    process, 142

questions relating to habits of mind
    for, 109–10
presentational knowing, 54
Preskill, S., 126–27
process reflection, 26
  in educators transformative
    process, 142
  questions for, 109
Professional and Organizational
    Development, 144
Progoff, I., 114
psycho-cultural assumptions, 16
psychological functions
  Jung defining, 64–65
  thinking, feeling, sensing and
    intuition as, 64–65
psychological habits of mind, 20–21
psychological profiles, 70–71
psychological type theory
  attitudes and functions of, 63–65
  constructivism in, 62, 63
  critical reflection and critical
    self-reflection in, 75
  differentiation in, 71–72
  discourse in, 74–75
  disorienting events and, 73–74
  extrarational transformative learning
    in, 76
  extraverted feeling in, 65–66
  extraverted intuition in, 66
  extraverted sensing in, 66
  extraverted thinking in, 65
  functions in, 64–65
  individual differences example of,
    134–35
  individuation in, 72, 73
  introverted feeling in, 68
  introverted intuition in, 69
  introverted sensing in, 68–69
  introverted thinking in, 67
  Jung on, 61–65
  Myers Briggs Type Indicator in, 65,
    103
  overview of, 77
  psychological profiles, 70–71

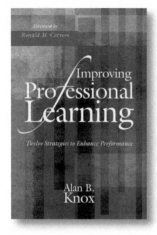

Improving Professional Learning
Twelve Strategies to Enhance Performance
Alan B. Knox
Foreword by Ronald M. Cervero

Given the tremendous importance of keeping up with the explosion of knowledge in professional fields—from medicine and health to teaching in schools and colleges—getting the most out of every learning opportunity is vital to the growth and vitality of our society, as well as to the development of professional practitioners themselves.

In this concise, practical guide to improving professional learning and performance, Alan B. Knox brings decades of experience and study to bear on 12 key tasks for the leader of professional learning activities. Illustrated with examples from a wide variety of learning settings across the helping professions (e.g., health care, teaching, social work), the chapters provide essential guidance to instructors and facilitators seeking to improve learning activities and thereby enhance professional performance. The combination of evidence-based concepts and practical examples is designed to enable readers to improve the learning activities they lead, enhancing the performance of learners in their ongoing professional practice.

Ronald M. Cervero, professor and associate vice president for instruction at the University of Georgia, writes in the foreword:

> Alan Knox has provided leadership for this important area of scholarship and practice for decades, and brings all of his insights, experience, and research to help educational leaders improve professional learning. The 12 strategies that form the heart of this book are essential elements for anyone providing professional learning, from starting where the learner is, through the focusing on active learning, and ending with providing feedback to learners and other stakeholders. Without a doubt, this book is a major contribution to support improved practice of professional learning and continuing professional education.

22883 Quicksilver Drive
Sterling, VA 20166-2102

Subscribe to our e-mail alerts: www.Styluspub.com

Also available from Stylus

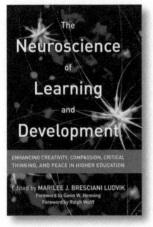

The Neuroscience of Learning and Development
Enhancing Creativity, Compassion, Critical Thinking, and Peace in Higher Education
Edited by Marilee J. Bresciani Ludvik
Foreword by Gavin W. Henning
Foreword by Ralph Wolff

Is higher education preparing our students for a world that is increasingly complex, volatile, and in which they will have to contend with uncertainty and ambiguity? Are we addressing the concerns of employers who complain that graduates do not possess the creative, critical thinking, and communication skills needed in the workplace?

This book harnesses what we have learned from innovations in teaching, neuroscience, experiential learning, and studies on mindfulness and personal development to transform how we deliver and create new knowledge and indeed transform our students, developing their capacities for adaptive boundary spanning.

Starting from the premise that our current linear, course-based, educational practices are frequently at odds with how our neurological system facilitates learning and personal development, the authors set out an alternative model that emphasizes a holistic approach to education. This approach integrates mindful inquiry practice with self-authorship and the regulation of emotion as the cornerstones of learning, while demonstrating how these align with the latest discoveries in neuroscience.

This book closes by offering practical ideas for implementation, showing how simple refinements in classroom and out-of-classroom experiences can create foundations for students to develop key skills that will enhance adaptive problem solving; creativity; overall well-being; innovation; resilience; compassion; and, ultimately, world peace.

Copublished with ACPA – College Student Educators International

(Continues on previous page)